THE ZAZAR
TRANSMISSIONS
PAGES FROM THE COSMOS

MARILYN GEWACKE, PH.D.

LUMINOUS MOON PRESS
BOULDER, COLORADO

Cover and interior layout and design by Carolyn Oakley,
Luminous Moon Design + Press

Painting of ZaZar by Vashta Narada

First Edition
First Printing: July 2021

Publication Data
Marilyn Gewacke
The ZaZar Transmissions: Pages From the Cosmos

ISBN-13: 978-1-7372637-1-5
Body, Mind & Spirit – Channeling & Mediumship –
UFOs & Extraterrestrials

Printed and bound in the United States of America

Table of Contents

Acknowledgments

I first must acknowledge and thank the two amazing stewards and curators of these extraordinary teachings of ZaZar, Diane Saunders and Jennifer Westacott. The many, many hours of time and inspiration they have given to ZaZar's steadfast streaming of brilliance and wisdom has been amazingly uplifting and heartening. I have watched them absorb and process the cosmic frequencies of ZaZar's tutelage… transforming and illuminating their consciousness and increasing the light and love they carry into the world…manifesting the reality of these pages. This has given me so much hope, fortitude and motivation to faithfully channel these remarkable, multifaceted transmissions. Diane, my beautiful cosmic beloved, has been exemplary in her magnificent mission for heralding and disseminating ZaZar's message on Earth at this time. Without her unending, gentle but fierce support, this book would not be possible nor would I. Magnificent light warrior, strong and determined, Jen Westacott has been and continues to be an illustrious champion of this mission and has remained an integral part in making this book possible by reading and refining the pages therein.

I want give a very special thank you to Karen Muñoz who was the prime editor of this book, spending many hours of reading, pondering and adding such beautiful suggestions. Her grace and humbleness in deciphering ZaZar's words, while adding to the fluidity of the sentences, was quite amazing. Much gratitude towards my creative publisher, Carolyn Oakley and Luminous Moon. Carolyn has wholeheartedly stayed with me through the editing, arranging and publishing of two books. The format, layout and cover are due to her artistic understanding of the material provided.

A big embrace of gratitude also goes to Vashta Narada, world-renounced visionary artist, who brilliantly and skillfully portrayed ZaZar's portrait on the back cover. Vashta's ability to travel in other dimensions and "see" and communicate with ET Beings is quite extraordinary. ZaZar's magnificent essences are beautifully alive when peering into his eyes and feeling his presence by simply seeing his image. This visual encounter opens our hearts and expands our consciousness…offering the experience of our own cosmic birthing.

In addition, I want to state my deep gratitude for the extraordinary, illuminated community at the Sanctuary for Evolutionary Vision (SEV). Collectively, they have dedicated enormous energy as students of ZaZar, accompanying him through meditative journeys, classrooms, retreats and even an amazing trek to the Georgian Bay in Canada. This community is truly the hope and revelation for the planet, demonstrating how the illuminated High-Heart can elevate who we are individually and, most importantly, who we can be as a fifth dimensional Community of Human Beings. This extraordinary community is the accelerator and glimmering catalyst for the evolution of human consciousness and the coming of the New Dawn on Earth.

I also want to thank those who have created the colorful brushstrokes in my life, giving me the opportunity to see the truth of my higher 5D self as they are reflected in me and I am in them. As I journey with ZaZar to the invisible realms, at times it has been difficult to bring back "proof" of these realities, however he has taught me that the proof is in the Being-ness of my personage. So, I know for absolute certainty that the invisible has become visible in who I am and how I live. Without those around me (both difficult and loving), I would not see that which I am bringing to Earth. This is true for all of us…how magnificent that the proof finally lies in the beauty of our hearts and the touch of our souls.

Most respectfully and joyfully, I want to thank ZaZar for his patient, gentle, humble and illuminating presence in my life. I have come to know ZaZar as not only my Earth teacher and mentor but part of my cosmic family as well. He has helped me see the truth of who I am, and the truth of who we all can be as a human species in the home of the Cosmic Universe. While ZaZar is an extraordinary Being of such high light magnitude, he is here only to inspire us to behold our own frequencies of the highest lighted way. ZaZar simply brings the New Age of the Fifth Dimensional Ascension to our doorstep, should we pause to open the door.

Marilyn Gewacke, Ph.D.
July 10, 2021
The Sanctuary

Prelude to the Awakening

We are experiencing a time in history that has never before happened. Something tremendous and magnificent is being ushered into our little planet called Earth. A new paradigm of fifth dimensional frequencies is coming upon us. The real issue is not whether *it* is here, but rather are *we* here in the consciousness of our higher selves and illuminated hearts. The good (and perhaps bad) news is that it is all up to us. We are at a beautiful turning point; through the mechanisms of cosmic free will, we can make choices to go where the human species has never been, at least on this planet Earth. It means new ways of thinking, feeling and being. We are headed into places and spaces that have not previously been conceived of by our civilization. It may feel a bit uneasy, doubtful and even perilously uncertain; however, it is exactly this unknowing that portends this birthing of the "Planetary Age of Ascension."

To truly experience the New Paradigms being birthed, one has to be willing to be courageous and daring enough to give up old notions of reality. We are indeed ready…are we willing? Open these pages without the old road maps of what you thought you knew and you will begin to see the outlines of this New Reality of Being. Feel the frequencies therein, and let them dance you to higher realms of universal wisdom and love. In the experience of this book, you will find yourself remembering the higher consciousness matrix of your soul. After all, you agreed to be a main player in its design! In the very reading of these pages, you become a co-creator of this New Paradigm of Ascension as you allow yourself to be in this vibratory experiential classroom. In doing so, you bring planetary hope and cosmic love (the fuel for the birthing) to yourself, all inhabitants of Earth and to Earth herself.

One thing I know for certain, **we** are the hope and it is **the** time for this fifth dimensional transformation of our Cosmic Consciousness. It will not look or feel like anything preconceived in our human thinking paradigm but will, instead, be birthed from the sacred soul designs from whence we came. This book opens those forgotten corridors and turns on the light of Cosmic Creative Design. I am finally feeling at home in these new landscapes of invisible vistas as I learn to see anew and hold the embrace of universal love and unity consciousness in the core of my very being. I hope this book helps you feel at home as well in the magnificent beauty of your soul's unfolding mission of Ascension on Earth.

Throughout this journey with ZaZar*, I indeed have been able to dissolve much of my old identity as Marilyn, and the various definitions that have formed the archival facts and fictions of my life. I understand now that, while these categories form normative guidelines that help us recognize where we belong and how to navigate life, they succeed in keeping us diminished and limited.

I no longer live in that place of chronicled ideations that rebound in the external world, but rather dwell in an experience created from the mystical, magical world "within" not without. Often, these experiences illuminate a lucidity where I slip out of time and space into a felt reality that gives birth to new sensory fields of seeing, feeling and knowing. What I have experienced now fuels the fire in the center of my being to follow these lighted strands of new, irradiated realities that lie in the invisible, yet now palpable, multidimensional realms.

---

*ZaZar is an extraordinary and beautiful sixth dimensional, extraterrestrial being that I have been channeling for the last five years.

It is our birthright to unfurl the very mapping in our DNA that will create the pathways to our lineage back to the stars where our souls live and our hearts fly on winged crafts of unimaginable worlds. I live in the experience of being more than the construct of a human being; the "what" of my being has become deliciously diminished as the "who" of my being further unfolds. This "wholeness" of being seems to be boundless, vast and measureless.

While these states can be uncomfortable to sit in, they have actually become my respite stations, my peace and my quiet, as I allow these novel vistas to take shape in unique domains of sensory experience. I have a deep knowing that this will someday be the avant-garde cosmic science, which will reveal the truth of our expanded powers for the miracles of healing, peace, love and true unity of consciousness. Perhaps it is the very lack of reinforcement and solutions from the world of old constructs and dualistic paradigms that gives me the fortitude and hope to explore this journey with the tenacity and spirit of those who will come after me. For they will walk in the certainty of these new realities, establishing new settlements of consciousness in the fifth dimensional (5D) realm.

I will forever be indebted to my beautiful mentor, teacher and escort, ZaZar, for having the patience to help me see through my own slumber and awaken to my own truth. If I am to be a good sojourner and student of the cosmic process, it is not only ZaZar I must thank, but our own enlivened free will, courage and amazing fortitude to explore the unknown boundaries of our spirited beings. In the end, while there is no doubt ZaZar provides the alchemy for such activation, I know this budding Cosmic Awakening into the Ascension journey is our opportunity to simply become the Magnificent Beings that we truly are.

I am fortunate enough to travel with an extended community of voyagers on this Earth plane who have come together to form a template of love, unity and amazing joy, giving hope that indeed we are most magnificent in our journey towards Oneness.

Chapter 1

Introduction

MARILYN'S PORTRAYAL

ZaZar came to me on July 16, 2016. Well, I should say that is my first channeled experience with him. I now know ZaZar has been with me throughout this lifetime. I was accustomed to receiving downloads of information…in what would seem a flash of a second. It would often take me several hours to reconfigure the information in such a way my three dimensional (3D) mind could recognize and understand. Sometimes the downloads would come in visual form, sacred geometry, musical notes or language. Yet, all the while, I knew I was working with a magical/mystical guide from multidimensional realms.

As a child, I received these messages but had no idea that this was not a common phenomenon. I wrote my first book, *The Oneness of Being: Birthing the New Human,* by deciphering many of these downloads. I felt ZaZar ever so close during this process of writing and a year after the book was published, ZaZar appeared through me as a channeled being. It has inexorably changed my life, shifting the tapestry of what and who I am. The new and transformational landscapes that I now walk are extraordinary and, at times, a bit mind-blowing. The one thing I know with absolute certainty is that ZaZar has taught me how to become a New Human with more compassion, grace and gratitude than ever before. I am learning to sustain that path with consistency and fortitude, even though at times I may waver and stray. I am grateful that I can remain more conscious of the swaying so that I find my way back with ease and knowingness. I write this book from ZaZar's transmissions, knowing that it is one attempt to aid us all on the Path of Ascension.

Before entering the halls of his cosmic libraries of wisdom, humor and teachings, it feels imperative to share what I know about this beautiful being called ZaZar. There are certainly many guides, celestial, interdimensional and extraterrestrial beings coming through to our planet now, sharing their extraordinary wisdom from the far reaches of and beyond space and time. What makes ZaZar so intriguing and mind-blowing to me is that his unique, cosmic teachings carry with them an amazing understanding of our human experience.

ZaZar's mission clearly is grounded and resonant with the current rhythms of frequency experiences on Earth at this particular time. He moves within the confines of the current human learning templates so that old constructs and debris programs vanish, making room with ease and comfort for the New Paradigm of Ascending transfiguration. It feels very much like a glove that perfectly fits the hand, neither too constricting nor too loose, but rather a sacred "hand-holding experience" with the assuredness of comfort and love. Information transforms and perfectly aligns within the confines of the human consciousness. As ZaZar shares his extraordinary wisdom, our awakening feels smooth and enlivening, touching some deep knowing within the human core that lights up with a harmonious and resonant experience. You can feel his ingenuity and gentleness as a deep burst of lighted, metaphoric remembrance-journey being birthed within.

Simply put, ZaZar is the most compassionate being I have ever encountered. It is a little intimidating to have such a wise High Being enter the corridors of my inner world. I realized very quickly that ZaZar knew much about my own debris fields, my imperfections and my areas of needed progress. Yet, I never once felt his disapproval, his judgment or disappointment. I see this with everyone he encounters. ZaZar seems to already know why we stumble, why we fall and why we come up short. It is simply part of why we have come.

ZaZar's understanding of the human paradigm lights the way for us to accept our foibles long enough to feel them and see the luminous way through them. He recognizes that which we have refused to acknowledge for fear we will be overwhelmed by our weakness, our frailties, our smallness. Instead, he leads us into those debris piles with loving hands so that we might free ourselves of this secreted, dense space we call the "egoic human self."

We have spent too much time in denial and amnesia. As a result, these gathered fields of debris still bear down on us and impede our spiritual lives. ZaZar has taught me that going through the field where my human inadequacies live is not a place of residence, but simply the road to expand out and up. He embodies the frequency of forgiveness, compassion and tremendous grace as he holds our human journeys with love and understanding.

My greatest desire is to be able to hold these same High-Heart frequencies within myself and with everyone else. I have watched ZaZar transform someone's journey with a slight touch of the hand, a smile of humorous proportions and a sentence of empathic and kind acceptance…all the while, his generosity of spirit and enormous patience are felt at every step. Within this sacred embrace, ZaZar prepares us for the Cosmic Teachings that irrevocably change our lives, catapulting us into the Ascension journey of fifth dimensional (5D) realities.

I have also learned that ZaZar teaches in a pyramidal style, which is most clever in assisting the human mind to slowly leave the visible, tangible world for the etheric world of the Cosmos. He first introduces ideas, information and frequency experiences on the bottommost materialized level of the pyramid. Once satiated with material knowledge of the human kind, ZaZar moves to the next level that takes up less material space, and begins to traverse beyond the tangible, corporeal world into higher, invisible frequency space. Each new level provides less earthly material, while moving into the world of higher consciousness and felt subtle frequencies.

The ticket for admission to each pyramidal layer simply requires you to be less human-formed and more spirit-consciousness permeated, thus making it possible to resonate in harmony with the new vibrational paradigms. The final elevation is the capstone of the pyramid pinnacle, which holds the least amount of material from the third dimensional realm yet carries the most expansive invisible frequencies of the multidimensional realms. And then…you are, once again, on the beginning stratum of some new pyramid, embracing the lands from which you came, readying yourself for flight with expanding wings, familiar and brand-new all at once.

ZaZar's transmissions are filtered through my own consciousness field, so I have tried to utilize human language in such a way to communicate his amazing, multidimensional frequencies. Downloads sometimes come in light language, sacred designs and sound movement, and so you might say that I am ZaZar's deciphering agent. Other times, I write his transmissions exactly as I hear them for he is amazingly adept at utilizing the poetic nature of our language.

ZaZar has made it abundantly clear that he wants the written word to sound familiar, at times opting for a colloquial style, a casual dialect if you will, in order to accelerate the ease by which we are able to utilize the circuitry of our "language units" in our minds. He often just converses with me in what appears to be an exchange of discernible everyday English language, surprising me with his comfort and ease at speaking in the vernacular and the "lingo" of our times. It is only later that I begin to decipher the extraordinary frequencies he bestows in the rhythm of his words. Whether through me, Marilyn, or ZaZar himself, the words have become a full symphony of vibratory transformation.

There are times when my human brain does not quite comprehend his beautiful teachings, and yet I know that I am digesting them on some deeper soul level. Let your own process be filled with curiosity, wonder and awe as ZaZar takes you on a cosmic journey through mysterious and wondrous lands…once familiar, yet far away. I realize now that his frequency signatures are both captivating and contagious, lighting up those same vibratory states of being that have been within all of us since the beginning of…well let's find out, shall we?

ZaZar's Portrayal

Beautiful Beings of the Lighted Way, come journey with me into the magical land of the All of You. Let your 3D mind rest for a while, after all your thinking self has spent a great deal of time and energy trying to figure it all out. It is time to experience the truth, rather than "mind" the truth. Silence the old paradigms of understanding so that you might travel into the land of your vibrational Cosmic Self. It is here that you will know, feel, intuit, taste, touch and see all else beyond your world of matter and form.

You have been great stewards of the Human World, navigating through the various tides and turns of your life. And yet, in the midst of it all, you continued to feel a deeper calling to know the truth of who and what you are. Nothing in this three dimensional world made complete sense because the wholeness of your higher self cannot be found in this life alone. You are so much more, yet the diminishing effect of Earth living has left you more empty than full, and less magnificent and beautiful than is the truth of your Cosmic Nature.

So let's travel together on the brightly lit Craft of Infinite Consciousness so that you might see the landscapes of your Soul Matrix where all frequencies of past, present and future live. How marvelous that we have the opportunity to take this journey together. Can you feel the excitement within the quantum spaces of your being? As you read the passages within, **feel** them more than decipher them. Even when your 3D mind gets in the way, know that the vibrations on the pages will still come through to you, stimulating your long-lost knowledge of the multiverse and the multidimensional realms.

You are a being of infinite frequencies experiencing, for a moment, form and matter. *This corporeal world is simply the jumping off point, a transport station if you will, embedded with the necessary lessons and trials that become the tickets to all other realities. Take this trip to the outer boundaries of your incarnate anatomy, structure and framework.* As you journey to the outer edges of your higher consciousness, you will begin to feel the vibrational nature of the Universe. It is in this place that you will experience these transmissions and, in that experience, you will know and begin to see into the vastness of the infinite, invisible realm beyond space and time. How could you refuse such an invitation?

You are so much more than this one incarnation. However, know that it is within *this* particular human form at this particular time, you have arrived in order to become a vibrational, fifth dimensional being, surpassing and transforming form and matter beyond space and time. Can you remember this agreement for this Ascended Mission? You are truly beautiful, cosmic and starlit, so let's take a ride on the wild side…opening your portals to all things and all times. Remember, you are a Frequency Being. Every time you open this book, this Cosmic Primer for you, pause to feel your vibrations and allow the rhythm and heartbeat of you to join and merge with the sacred pulse that lies within these pages. This will amplify your frequency quotient, lifting you into the quantum realm where everything lives and breathes.

Thank you for joining me and many others, and know from this point on we will be traveling together on Earth and in the Stars. Realize that every word holds the vibrations of starlit energy, but most importantly begin to feel the space in between…for the frequency therein unlocks the All of Everything. Stay open, breathe deeply and become the Truth of Who You Are.

Chapter 2

The Who of ZaZar

I understand that it is important to identify who I am, for in human realities the identification process seems to help with safety and potential affability and congeniality. So, I will relay some things that might help you feel the contours of who I am; however, these things that I will be telling you will no doubt create, what you call, "cognitive dissonance." The third dimensional mind is a sticky place, full of habits and captive realities. The best place to start is to tell a story from a different place and time…a different Being. Otherwise, I would do a disservice to begin in the familiar world of your mind, where you will stay confined and reduced. As it is, I do not live in that world, so how could I start where I do not live? Come with me into a world beyond your world…stay open to the fullness and delightfulness of these expanded and (for the moment) unimaginable realities.

I am a sixth dimensional (6D) extraterrestrial being. Just pause to feel that and you will awaken to your own beauteous Cosmic Pixels of light within! I have come here now to assist in the fifth dimensional Ascension process on Earth through Frequency Recognition and Experiential Technology. Sounds big? Yes, you are right. It is BIG. Please know it is not BIG because of me, it is BIG because of you. You have called for many of us to come now…you are ready and it is a Universal Covenant that when there is a readiness for Cosmic Transformation, sustenance and guidance shall be sent! ♡ *Heart Note Pause* *(see page 20)*

And so I am here. I am actually a sixth dimensional being, more formless than formed. However, in order to channel to a third dimensional being, I stepped down into a fifth dimensional body, a body being that is very familiar and beautiful to me. You might say an incarnation I am living at the same moment of my sixth dimensional beingness. As a fifth dimensional being, I am Arcturian, Pleiadian and Elfin ET. You see, in the 5D realities you can learn how to choose your "Cosmic DNA."

I chose these three cosmic configurations, as it created a mission template for me, so that I could honor and uphold my Star commitment to come to Earth for this auspicious time of unfoldment. Someday humans will learn to decipher and choose what DNA to turn on or off (right now it is mainly unconscious). You will also learn that some genetic codes no longer serve the purpose of your higher consciousness and, therefore, make room for galactic downloads of new Cosmic Codes of dimensional transformation. For now, suffice it to say that we in the Cosmos have the ability to design our Cosmic Genesis Codes. This certainly makes for a lively Universe of amazing, diverse beings. I must say that many of you wonder why ETs do not make themselves more known. Can you imagine coming to a planet where you see the beautiful diversities of a species, yet you see them destroying each other because of those very diversities? Until you can hold your own beauty within your species, it is very difficult for many of us to think you can handle the enormous diversities of the Universe.

My sixth dimensional, incarnate self comes from the Zoridium Star System. You will find this by locating the Cepheid Stars directly

---

HEART NOTE PAUSE: When you see this Heart Note Pause throughout the book, take a moment for a brief respite, a "breathing space" if you will. Pausing provides for the "in-between" moment for reaching into other dimensions and realities. In the pause, the frequency makes itself known providing a slipstream into tangible realms of consciousness. Heart Note Pauses are the 5D version of footnotes…thus referencing the inner world wisdom rather than the outer world libraries.

opposite Earth in the outermost spiral of the Milky Way galaxy from Earth. I have spent much time on an ET Elfin planet in this beautiful Zoridium Star System. It is quite an extraordinary 5D planet with Merlin Magic and Mystical Patterns of Sacred Design. Life forms become more and more complex as you expand in the Ascension Cone and, all at once, simplified in Light Design. By the way, eventually you can't identify any one specific DNA contribution in material form as the Soul becomes Whole in Conscious Revelation. And in the higher dimensions, there is less and less form and more light. This lighted, vibrational, sacred design originates from Divine Source and so you become more Source and less form, until…can you begin to imagine?

I am part of a Galactic Star Corps living on a beautiful, extraterrestrial craft above Earth. We are from many civilizations and represent a beautiful combination of metamorphic healing, transformational frequencies from many parts of the Multiverse. We are here for you now. Each Being carries special responsibilities, gifts and assets for Earth, her inhabitants and the entire solar system you reside in. Your Earth is in a time of great change and the call has gone out. Pause once again to feel this truth. If you try to think it, you will become trapped in the smallness of your 3D mind. Feel it, imagine it…and so it will be that you will come to know us, but most importantly know You. ♡

I would like you to know that we have studied and become quite intimate with the workings of the human species and Earth for quite some time, so that we may be of service now; however, it is not the same studying that you might do. Yes, we know and explored your history (not necessarily the history you have been taught), your cultures, your art, your music, your expressions, etc. This helps us understand how you think, how you feel and, most importantly, how you assimilate the frequencies created by your species. Your frequency states, as expressed in words, actions, thoughts and feelings, are most important for us to understand, for it is in this way I have learned how to communicate with you in a manner that can be received and digested. In studying your "frequency receptor systems," I was able to decipher how to communicate in your vibratory language to harmonize and create convergence with your internal habitat. For example, many of your own telepathic channels are closed or only partially opened, and so I have had to master speech and voice communication because communication in the Fifth Dimension is mainly through telepathic means. Even so, there are beautiful frequencies imbedded in my voice and in my words that speak to your awakening consciousness.

At times, I will use language to name things unfamiliar to you, like our planets, star systems, various civilizations, etc. It is not that these words per se are the pronouncements of our language, but rather an extrapolation of the frequencies that might transfer to the sounds and feelings of the words that you utilize. It is always the vibratory nature of the sound that is important, as the rhythmical notes of the word simply open the door or portal to awaken your heart's cosmic pulse and the sacred geometry of higher consciousness. This should come with a warning…your 3D mind will not comprehend that which is held sacredly within these pages, so please be careful not to tax it. (Just a bit of humor.) On another note, it is most important to understand that nothing can be received without your complete free will agreement for such transmissions. I communicate through these words, but my true gift is the frequency embedded within. Pause once more to feel this. ♡

Your expressions and the nuances of your language are also crucial. We have discovered that often what you say and what you actually feel are two different things. Also, because you are only now coming into a new phase of consciousness realization, you still keep many things hidden in the backdrop of your awareness. And so, communication is tricky and sometimes rather absurd and opaque. Even before this channeling expression began, I had recognized that Earth humans live in a space where safety and trust are still being desperately sought, but yet unrealized. It has only been since I have been here among you and experienced the "living feeling frequencies" through the channeling that I have realized the extent to which you hold so much strife and struggle in your Earth journeys. It has only increased my respect and sacred embrace of the human journey, for it is more arduous and difficult than any of us knew. You are heroes in our world. *You have agreed and committed yourselves to such an amazing soul pilgrimage in a world that is unforgiving of the very debris and darkness you must encounter for Ascension Realization.*

Before delving into the Pages from the Cosmos, it is most interesting to note my relationship with Marilyn, who has agreed and committed to this sometimes exhausting yet exhilarating role as channeler. I have been with Marilyn all of her life, even before this life. You could say I have been waiting for her consciousness to reach a 'peak' level of transparency and frequency. She has finally arrived. Over the years, Marilyn has experienced many downloads of cosmic proportions and has learned to decipher them as she has intensified her own consciousness journey. She also had many experiences in our craft when she was a child, and is beginning to recognize and remember much of this. Of course, this is not always easy to embrace, let alone make apparent in the human world where she spends some of her time. I am most certain that the channeling process itself will bring her more peace than unrest, for I often say, "If you're not in the frequency of truth, you create a vibratory field of concealment that diminishes the 'lighted one' in the very core of your being." We have also experienced important incarnations together, where I was her teacher and "cosmic father." So you see, we have a shared lineage. This is important to know because it helps explain our close connection, the ease by which I can come through, and the truth and knowledge that Marilyn holds, enhancing her ability to channel. After the removal of egoic and specific incarnate motivations, her ability to channel has become easier and smoother, where she can experience both tranquility and exhilaration all at once during the channeling moments. Most importantly, she has learned to be a clear conduit with integrity and fortitude of mission. As you read the pages ahead, perhaps you can begin to experience the vibratory field of safety and trust in her, our mission and myself. *Know there is a perfect synchronistic rhythm between us that allows the frequencies from the multidimensional realms to dance on the pages and sing to your heart.*

Chapter 3

The Human Experiment

THE WHO OF THE HUMAN RACE

It is most important to realize and truly understand who you are and what you have come here to do. Your consciousness has been veiled and shrouded by the human experience. For some, it happened immediately; for others the remembrances remained intact until the Human Programs took priority. You accepted the daunting task to come here to be and do as a human. This is a laboratory of sorts…this human experience. You had to initially become absorbed in the human domain so that you could learn to navigate, becoming familiar with this reality…gaining wisdom about how to survive and eventually thrive. In order to truly know how to navigate the human 3D experience, you went through a period of amnesia, a fugue state if you will, where your Cosmic Self (the Soul Matrix of the All of You) was resting in a dormant place or aspect of your higher self. This enabled you to learn what it means to be human. In that process, however, many of you began to believe that indeed the only thing you are is contained in this human incarnation. You had to be in the totality of "being human" to know the landscapes and twists and turns of this 3D reality. Becoming accustomed and acquainted with this new homeland was crucial from the very beginning. Otherwise, as you encountered the struggles of this life, you might have made your stay very brief!

The plan was for deep memories of your cosmic self and mission to become resurrected and aroused. In addition, the "soul essences" that you brought with you would once again be activated and reawakened. The very act of this awakening would spawn frequencies that would create a tremendous light wave, opening all that you truly are. In that moment, you would begin the arduous process of uncovering these multidimensional truths of who you are and what you have come to do! Your higher/cosmic self was well aware that coming to Earth to "be" human and keep the soul fires burning beneath the surface of the 3D experience could be a very tricky, risky and precarious process. Can you begin to see how magnificent, powerful and light-filled you must be to come to such a task on Earth? We praise and cheer you with Starlight applause and hold you in such high esteem for opening to this momentous, remembrance journey.

Unfortunately, no one knew exactly what the state of affairs was on Earth at the time of your arrival. As free will is always the guiding principle, the dominant species of any particular planet determine the evolving process of Ascension. When you arrived here, the darkness was almost at a catastrophic level and Earth herself was struggling to stay alive and well. We had hoped that the Earth Planet Celestial Being would be able to support both your awakening and the new frequencies coming into the Earth. Sadly, the state of the 3D frequencies had solidified so much that not only were they harming the planet, but also creating cloaks and borders so dense and impenetrable that awakening seemed almost impossible for so many. These shrouds became heavy and burdensome and the cosmic memories were lost in the heavy fog of 3D living. For many, the veils actually became the identity…a paradox of sorts was created. Only the ground crew (you) could truly assess the condition of the human species and the planet, and yet it was this very condition that blinded your ability to "see" yourself, your surroundings and your mission. The good news is that many of you are indeed waking up…and because of that, we are here to help you quicken this process! Can you begin to see why we hold you in such splendid reverie as we see how dedicated you are in blasting through the human debris fields in order to come "back home" to the truth of your cosmic origins and your cosmic contracts? Often when light is birthed through the darkness, it causes a huge ripple effect, not only throughout your planet but throughout the Cosmos as well. So, you might see why your awakening is something to be witnessed and celebrated. *Every enlightened moment creates a birthing of Source Frequencies pulsating and flowing out into the Universe...expanding the experience of Source "isness."*

There are certain things written in the Cosmic Chronicles about all possibilities, wavelengths, dimensions and realities. You are part of the prophesied progeny who would come to Earth to help her ascend and transmute the furies of lower dimensional energy. As in all records and destiny paths, there are many possibilities due to the free will of all those who come. You, and you alone, are the determinant of your future awakenings. What an absolutely exciting and glorious task! We, higher dimensional ET beings, are also part of this and our cosmic contract involves holding your awakening with unconditional love in order to see the precise moment when your hearts begin to dance in the light of this cosmic dream. We are joyously here to aid and assist in this activation process. As previously mentioned, this will have ripple effects throughout the Cosmos. We thank you for allowing us to be part of this most amazing Ascension Creation. So you see, you have both a ground crew and a cosmic crew...this is the first stage of the "Oneness Operation." Do you understand what that means? So, let's get started. Your cosmic dance has begun!

It is important to know that many souls now arriving in this Earth plane have been equipped with mechanisms that will keep their memories closer to the surface, as they will have less veils, less burdens and less amnesia as a result of *your* work. And, because of the work many of you have already done and are doing, a new pool of generated frequencies on Earth has been created for the "new ones" to bathe in. As wild as this may sound, you have given permission and have been transmitting your experience to us since your arrival. That data and information has been utilized to help the new arrivals, and they have been "fitted" with certain cosmic keys to counter the 3D amnesia that most have encountered. You can see and feel how different they are… ready and waiting for you to open up the portals of Ascension Energy.

First, you must understand and fully know the blocks and debris fields you are up against. The 3D field is alive and well, keeping itself moving yet firmly anchored within the Earth domain. Dimensional realities are living entities just like planets and stars are beautiful Celestial Beings. Every being wants to survive and thrive. This is how Source continues to create. Every planet, every star and every dimension is a different **Being** depending on where it lives and how it is sourced. Earth has a particular Celestial Being that agreed to come and become this beautiful, living presence called Gaia. As with all beings, free will is woven into the essence or fabric of each living entity. *Free will is essential because only that consciousness, residing in each being, can know the experience of the Ascending process and decide to move in the direction of actualizing the cosmic codes within.* The 3D space and time you live in is also a living consciousness that has qualities of the archetypal Third Dimension and the individual qualities of where it has been placed in space and time. In this case, Earth has danced with the third dimensional frequencies for quite some time. She is now tasked with ascending into a fifth dimensional reality. The gravitational pull of 3D programs, and time and space anchors, are holding on for dear life. Soon they will become the very fuel for the explosion of light on your planet as Ascension stirs her fires for expansive realization.

Suffice it to say, part of your own difficulties in ascending with Gaia has to do with the storminess and, at times, moodiness of the 3D paradigm. Humans have such a tendency to personalize struggles, often blaming themselves for their slow progress and painful transitioning. If you knew what you were up against, you would sing praises to yourselves, exalting your beautiful mission of Awakening. Can you begin to hear the chorus from our ships? Open to the symphony of renewed frequencies…we are here!

So what must you do to get ready for this ride into fifth dimensional living and the New Earth? **Attention, Recognition, Acceptance and Action.**

ATTENTION & RECOGNITION: There have been several programs developed by the simple nature of surviving on this planet. Some programs have been purposefully planted and you, all on your own, have created others. Paying *attention* to these programs enables you to *recognize* them as they are triggered and played out in the dramas of your human incarnation. Once recognized, the liberating task of dissolvement and transmutation can take place.

So let's begin to explore some of the old paradigm programs that have been bestowed upon you to keep you confined in the 3D reality of Earth.

KEEPING THE STATUS QUO

Some of the frequencies of third dimensional reality have become separate from the All of Everything and have created mechanisms to keep the 3D intact and functioning in this disengaged consciousness. It might appear that these vibratory states of awareness are not conducive to the Awakening Process. However, awakening from the land of slumbered separation creates expanded light frequencies and is simply part of the great Cosmic Experiment. The Universe expands by "conscious created awakening" from Source (the All of Everything) within Source (You). On Earth, this awakening is the beginning of the Ascension transformation towards fifth dimensional living. There are indeed forces that see the power and magnificence of you and have come to bring Cosmic Consciousness to the planet. Yet these lower, denser frequencies have created many programs to block the truth of who you are. They do so in order to keep the current paradigm intact and fully functioning. Understand that, in many instances, this is not done with malice of heart or dark intention but rather a way to simply keep the status quo, just as you might go to war to keep yourselves and your families alive or even to keep your perspective or side the winner of some perceived contest. You see this everywhere on Earth...one species (humans) surviving at the expense of so many other species dying, or one political party, one country, one culture trying to survive even at the risk of destroying others. What individual realities or beings frequently forget is that we are all part of the WHOLE, not separate or apart. Especially in the 3D...because dualism is one of the mechanisms that keeps the third dimensional reality intact. It's "this or that" or "good or bad" and so on. The inevitable conclusion is, "If I am going to survive, something else has to go." That is not the truth of the Divine Matrix...for as dualism fades, higher dimensions are experienced. When you give the breath of life to just the parts and parcels in the Third Dimension, your memory of the larger Universal Whole Consciousness becomes shrouded and obscured. While you might forget, it is important to hold the beautiful truth that dualism is actually a way for Divine Source to see its varied parts and particular attributes. The ability to see and encounter the varied components of reality is a wonderful opportunity in the Third Dimension. And the ability to experience the blending of those separate parts, undulating into a beautiful mosaic of frequencies, creates the alchemic process whereby some new harmonious entirety is felt. You might say that the cataclysmic mixing of polarities births the Wizard within you that waves the wand of transformation, birthing the totality of frequencies for the Fifth Dimension.

This is one of the most important paradoxes to understand and experience. You were given an ego/self to guide this process of becoming human and in that journey took seriously the idea that you were separate and alone. The survival of the fittest took control of your planet and the ego took control of your journey. This helped keep your cosmic origins and mission at bay so that you could survive this human journey. Little did you know you were not human; it was just the vehicle you were in to gather crucial information about the New Paradigm to come. Let me repeat the Paradox of this Human

Incarnation: *You have chosen to become human to bring humanity to the next step of evolution.* In order to gather the information necessary for this mission you had to be totally immersed in this experience, even when it meant you had to fight others for individual survival. Yet this very immersion clouded memories of your total Oneness with Source and your Cosmic Multidimensional Self. Quite a dilemma! So you see that maintaining the status quo becomes paramount to surviving and thriving; it is where safety and "knowingness" lives. If you know the parameters for survival that are found outside yourself, then you will subsist and endure the arduous journey of human living. A subtle but powerful message emerges from deep within…to "stay in what is known and you will gather what is necessary to succeed and even prosper." You will then be invulnerable within the walls of the self-created idea of your 3D sanctuary. Unfortunately, as you spend energy maintaining this kind of status quo, it becomes more like an asylum for separated souls and no longer a sanctorum of peace and expansion. *The willingness to stand outside the box and focus your mental and spiritual acquisitiveness to behold the unknown is a cosmic prerequisite for the classroom of Ascension Realities.* You have built much of your life on what is known. It is time to let the calling whispers of the invisible realms resound and rumble within so that you may begin to recognize and attend to your own "soul/cosmic voice." Let it become a thunderous chorus of the sweet notes of remembrance! It is quite a celebratory day when a Being realizes they can thrive as an exquisite, individual spark of the Cosmic Matrix, all the while knowing the truth of Oneness and Co-Creation. In fact, the more you feel the beautiful fabric of your Cosmic/Soul Matrix, the more joy you will experience from Divine Source. Soon the Golden Figure Eight will be alive and well within the Cosmic Structure of your DNA.

Again I want to emphasize that these mind control creations have not necessarily come from evil intention, although certainly there are entities that have ulterior motives to create fear, chaos and darkness. Many of those factions have simply taken their job too seriously, separating themselves from the light. This leads to one of the most important starting points: *Do Not Concern Yourself with the Darkness...* stay in your own light. The more curious you are about the outside darkness, the more inroads you open for the darkness to resonate with your inquisitiveness, worry and fear, thereby infiltrating your entire being. The best way to understand the larger entities of darkness that prowl Earth is to simply understand the darkness you hold within. It is different only in your mind's eye because that is your way of distancing yourself from the hidden debris you have concealed for decades. Once you understand the darkness within, you have all the tools necessary for dismantling the darkness externally. Remember, you have come here to discover the All of what is here on Earth at this time. The only way to know what is here is to be here...that is why you know more than we can know about the current human experiment. And so, it is also true that the way to know about the dark is to experience, house and sometimes become the dark. Do not condemn yourselves; simply become objective detectives in the laboratory of your human experience. As you awaken, the light frequency quotient will increase and your denser veils will dissolve.

PERSONALITY

When you first enter an incarnated body, your consciousness matrix can be totally intact and aware. You are still in the unity matrix of the All of You...all wisdom gathered, all frequencies experienced, all lives lived, all parts recognized as part of the Whole/Holy you. As consciousness begins its acquaintance with human form, the nature of space and time in this form begins to capture segments of the fires of awareness. This is crucial for you as you develop recognition of a new navigation system in order to move through this unfamiliar incarnated world. You begin to navigate through the principles and program guides in the human world...taking them on, trying them on and wearing them so that you might see and know the macro and microcosms of this Earth world. As you do this, *your awareness becomes* *more streamlined into the third dimensional human domain and you become so absorbed **in** the world that you begin to forget that you are not **of** it.* Attachments form to this incarnation and, sooner than later for most, you lose memory of the lighted self as this incarnation itself becomes your reality.

As you think and feel within the parameters of these protocols and "ground" rules, various programs and guides of this human 3D zone begin to form your personality. These personalities develop and become the vehicles that carry these self-describing ideas and feelings of your newly incarnated world. In this process, you slowly lose touch with the more expansive cosmic you. Although, you must have these experiences, as they are the foundation from which Ascension takes place, your awareness becomes constricted and restricted in this human world and the "higher you" is forgotten, along with why you have come here. *You might say, as the personality forms, the lighted consciousness of you dims and your awareness shifts to the necessary idea of who you are as "human" and how to move through its somewhat complex maze.* Third dimensional protocols have been given for how to act as a particular gender, race, ethnic group, cultural group, educational group, family, and the list goes on and on. For survival, you incorporated these into the structure of personality and operate as if that is who you are. Many of you have mirrored reflections (many times inaccurately) of certain human attributes, such as shy, smart, average, etc. These constructs become solidified into the form of you and conscious awareness then becomes glued to these rather unmoving experiences. As you become attached to these formulations, the lighted consciousness of the All of You wanes and diminishes. The experience and knowing of your Magnificence and Beauty shrink…lying await in a small, holding tank of dormant remembrance.

ACCEPTANCE & ACTION

STEP INTO THE TRUTH OF YOU

First step: Understand you are *not* your personality. It has only been a vehicle to take you through life experiences so that you might navigate the lands of this particular human incarnation. It is time to give up the keys to this vehicle in order to discover the forgotten passkeys to the dominion of your Ascendant Self. After all, this is why you have come… to be this ascending higher self, holding this Source-sparked lighted consciousness in human form! Take a brief pause to Remember. This opens the deeper truth of you who are…quite magnificent! ♡

Second step: Stay aware and awake to this truth so that you become an astute and diligent shamus to unearth the various triggers of diminishment and denial of this "true you." Your personality has developed the tricky, sticky trappings of the old order of you and so will be quite steadfast in providing the main voice that determines what you believe, experience and do. Commitment to giving room to the whispers from this deeper place of soul source must be strident and strong as you are so much more than your told stories, history, habits and patterns. These are simply the earthly designs within your personality so that you might experience the human incarnation fully and wholeheartedly. In this process, however, many of you accomplished it with such gusto you began to believe this is all there was. And yet, there was a hushed sigh within that said, "There is so much more." Yes? Yes! If you are reading these pages, you have already rounded that corner and see these words as the reflection of that expanding dimension of You.

Third step: Develop a Mantra to redirect your awareness and consciousness to the expanding you. Perhaps it is something simple like, "I am more than my personality. I am more than this incarnation." Perhaps, if you feel especially strong and ready: *I am the All of Everything I have ever been in all incarnations, parallel lives, essences and cosmic codes within* *the Matrix of my Divine Soul!* I suggest you go for this gusto (dilly-dally no more!) and begin the process of experiencing this lighted place within your matrix. In doing so, you begin to open the essences, codes and remembrances you came to Earth to materialize in the grand matrix of ascending into the 5D Domain.

No need to delay the totality of the birthing experience of waking up in the light of soul consciousness within the sacred design of this incarnated form. You have come here for just this Mission! This waking process produces a ripple effect that is felt across the Universe. Make no mistake about this.

What a magnificent Mission you have chosen! *So remember, your personality is but a small cog in the wheel of Ascended Motion. It is time to spin this wheel from the Seat of the All of You.*

DOUBT

One way to keep the old paradigm alive is to develop programs that help humans *doubt* all other possible paradigms! I am quite aware that as you read these pages, your agendas of doubt, apprehension and disbelief will rear up in great magnitude. For you have been conditioned to believe that comfort, safety and satisfaction arise out of the current belief systems, whether they originate in religions, cultures, communities, families or teaching institutions. Remember, those systems are engaged in keeping the status quo, which in turn will keep order, structure and those very systems intact. This makes sense, but clearly keeps your consciousness stifled and strangled so that you might not see the Light Horizon of Source and may not feel your cosmic memories awakening. *It is crucial to remember that your most inalienable right is to surpass, eclipse and exceed your current prison of 3D realities.* It is time to take up the sword of Light Activation and know the truth that is far beyond your current imagination. Remember the energetic field of doubt is, by far, the heaviest veil shielding your vision, dampening your spirit and eroding your life force energy. Doubt keeps you running in place, while faith and courage fuel you to leap. Doubt also makes you stay within the confines of the old paradigm where everything is known and the data has been gathered. Perhaps you must ask yourself, "Why would I stay in such a stagnant place where nothing is born anew…for safety, for surety, for certainty?" Choosing the path of "what is already known" is surely the path of death to the birth of the Cosmic Self. The paradox is that you have been programmed to look outside yourself for what is known and documented as real; yet, the only place for you to really know the "truth" is your world within. And in this place lies the infinite "data" of all things created by Source! *Look with the inner eyes of Lighted Consciousness and you will behold Source Consciousness in everything surrounding you.*

As you lift the veils of doubt, you will begin to "see" beautiful vistas in the multidimensional realm of All That Is. It will look differently, feel differently, taste differently, sound differently, and slowly you will begin to think differently. Entering a new reality will certainly alter and rock your worldview. You may feel dizzy, shaky, befuddled and bewildered at times, but I guarantee you will never be bored or stifled or subdued by this inward process of throwing off the old and stepping into the new world of wonder and beauty. You have come here to be a Cosmic Warrior. **Believing this** is your biggest challenge.

So practice this: put aside your old beliefs of everything you have thought so far and, just for a brief moment, imagine that you indeed are a Cosmic Sojourner. You have come to Earth to be in a human experience, so that you might understand firsthand what it means to be human. You are truly a Cosmic Being with infinite mystical and magical powers of great vision and Source Connection. You are here to help the Earth ascend and transform and, in that process, assist the human species in becoming a multidimensional species of peace, joy and love. You have simply fallen asleep so that you might totally "know" the human experience. You had to forget your higher/cosmic self so that you would know the experience of humanness, and you did this well. Now it is time to Wake Up! In this waking up, self-doubt will rear its head, but that is because the egoic self will want to survive. How wonderful to want to survive!

It is imperative to understand the powerful role of doubt, for it has been in place to keep you from your Grandness and your Magnificence. Yet another paradox: the egoic self desires "grand" reflection from the outside world by keeping its separation intact. However, in doing so, it isolates itself from the connective cosmic matrix of the All of You, where your magnificent light lives and breathes the holy communion with your multidimensional self. As you wake up to this expansive truth of the infinity of you, you will doubt and distrust its merit as you look upon this from your human-designed programs. Even as you begin to see the beauty and wonderment of your lighted, beautiful soul self, the automated protocol of doubt will immediately send waves of distrust, fear, disillusionment and disbelief about the truth of your power, strength, beauty and lighted magnificence. Unfortunately, there have been many in your life who would gladly diminish this realization for you. It is the law of separation, disparity and dualism of your 3D world where it has been said that there can't be room for all to be this Grand. This is only bestowed upon a relegated few. Of course, this is not the Law of Source Ascension. *For in Unity Consciousness, the All of All creates the light of all creation.* In your old dualistic world, it would seem impossible for the coexistence of the human and the Cosmic Self, but in this New Age of multidimensional realities, All can be at once. So you see, in this awakening process, it is imperative to preserve the Human Heart so that it might beat with the rays of cosmic light and form the New Cosmic Human! Your High-Heart knows the truth of you…holding it for this moment.

Release the doubt that lies in wait in the circuitry of your old mind fields, for doubt is only an obstacle to the portals opening to the invisible realms where all else lives and breathes. After all, is it not much more enticing and astonishing to birth the unknown into the known, thus expanding the world of consciousness in the Universe of Divine Source? I might add, the human race seems rather stuck in repeating the known…totally forgetting the power of the invisible worlds that lie just outside of current constructs. Limiting consciousness to the proverbial known paradigms limits expansion, repeating destructive patterns, mistakes and old misgivings. *Sadly, in its wish to preserve itself, the human race clearly has dwindled planetary life sustainment, combusting into pieces of debris and disillusionment the very resources that might save you.* You might say, the very life breath of your species is withering and waning. No fear or doubt, for this is all part of the Ascension process of dimensional transitioning. The old breaks apart to create more than the sum of the parts parlayed. So what appears unknown now is simply the known breaking apart, making room for the new frequencies of the coming dimensional shift. *Your willingness to walk on the bridge to nowhere with your inner beauty, strength and faith is the beginning of creating the new "elsewhere" where the invisible becomes seen and the new voice within becomes heard.* It is then that you will know that all along this "elsewhere" was waiting in the wings of the Synchronistic Divine Web. It is You who will manifest and create this new metamorphic frequency, fueling the rise of the Fifth Dimension on your planet called Earth. *You are the Ones to bring this incredible Ascension process into fruition, bearing the fruit of Source frequencies through the potency to manifest the light essence of your Soul Matrix through Conscious Consecration.* See this blessing! This is your mission...your divine free will to co-create, once again, the manifestations of "light in form" for universal expansion. So what do you say? Can you let go of the quagmires of the languishing status quo, the dwindling life force of the resident personality and the diminishing and denser frequencies of doubt, to become the flowering nectar of Sacred Design in and out of form? What a marvelous Sacred Design...You!

THE WHAT: The Ascension Journey

As you become Conscious of who you really are and come more fully into the Light of Cosmic Awareness, *what*, then, will you be up to? You will be on a most magical and mystical voyage of astronomical proportions! Know that the process of Ascension is happening everywhere in the Multiverse. It is the movement of light seeking light, creating and expanding the All of Source. When Ascension occurs in the materialized planes (on planets and in the forms of beings), it is a process whereby materialization comes to know itself both as Source Spark and the unique design of Soul Inspiration. You might say it is the "calling home" of the frequencies of light that are you. Your Universe is ever-expanding as a result of the Ascension process and you are part of the co-creation of this expansion. Take in this wonderful metaphoric vision for you. *As Divine Source exhales its sacred design into every material manifested form that includes you, the All of Everything patiently waits for you to inhale this sparked magnificence, thus crystalizing your lighted consciousness into awareness while in form.* In the domain of your free will, you can begin to exhale this celestial spark into the everything surrounding you. You see how the beautiful Golden Figure 8 comes into action...you with Source breathing the expansive Ascended Frequency Templates... expanding the never-ending flow of co-creation. How amazing! How beautiful! How magnificent! You see, you are part of this Ascension process whereby you, by your very awareness of the truth of who you are, transforms and upgrades the light frequencies on your planet. *At the level of the Third, Fourth and Fifth Dimension, Ascension is simply the metamorphic process by which the material world becomes permeated with Conscious Awakening, creating the buoyancy of lighter frequencies, thus escaping the gravitational pull of the denser planes.* These creative manifestations potently dance towards Divine Source, enabling the expansive burgeoning breathing of the Golden Figure 8 into many divergent sacred Universes, ever spinning the Ascended Energies into infinity. You see how magnificent you are to be the light-breathing dancer in this spinning lighted Universe of yours...where your lighted Soul Matrix has birthed many lives, many times, many places? You are here, right now on this Earth plane, to know this and be this, and in so doing create the fuel for the Earth to join its cosmic neighbors in fifth dimensional living. This will spawn and birth light for all generations to come in your Cosmic Galactic Home. Don't you think it's just a little bit exciting?

THE WHERE: Earth—The Shifting Field of Ascension

First of all, it has to be understood that to be on Earth at this time is absolutely an astounding opportunity. It is a singular and remarkable occurrence in your galaxy, as your Earth enters the rings of Ascension at the pinnacle of the Cosmic Turn. This is the point at which the balance of one dimension tips into the elevated reality of the next dimension. This is occurring on Earth right now. Do not mistake the chaos on your planet as a sign that you are sinking into the abyss, but rather a definite sign of the process of metaphoric transfiguration that is transpiring now. For the balance of the old 3D paradigm has most certainly become "topsy-turvy" and is reeling out of control. The stuck frequency states that occur in the Third Dimension have solidified into the dense impediments that hold you captive. The good news is that they are coming to an end. You are experiencing more and more moments of the Fourth Dimension, where the polarities of your Third Dimension are crashing together and becoming bits and pieces. They are losing their previous cemented forms and shapes. This can feel a bit crazy, staggering and whirling, creating a vertiginous experience. Although this period is not for the faint-hearted, you have come to be the bold and strong-hearted. Don't you feel that even in your moment of sadness and darkness?

Rest assured that chaos is to awaken you…to enliven and shake open your memories. Would you change a thing if not for disruption and the darkness of injustice and derision? Yes, it is a momentous signal to clear out debris fields and lower frequency experiences, feelings and thoughts. You cannot ascend without letting go of the dense anchors that keep you suspended in the lower vibrations that arise out of polarized living and the diminishment programs that abound in your Earth plane. You also must feel the chaos, for it is the rumbling sign of this new Reality birthing itself! There is nothing in the Universe at the 3D level that doesn't rumble and rock and roll before the dawning of a new era.

It is crucial to understand that doubts and fears are like "gravity spinners" holding you back from higher flight. It is always a bit disconcerting to enter unknown realms, but it is your mission to do so! It is in this higher flight that new realities and vistas can be seen. The horizon of the next rung of vertical rise is just above your current weight. Let go of some of what tethers you...your worries, your obsessions, your addictions, your old safety coping-thinking patterns. Do not waste energy on seeking out 3D solutions or pathways, for the new reality passageways do not lie in any paradigm you already know. If it did, you would already be there! Instead, be prepared to fly into the unknown...we are there and will assist you, but it is you that must leap. Chaos and discomfort are simply catalysts and part of the alchemic process necessary to move you to a new era. It is both a sign and motivator...evidence, if you will, that the pot is being stirred. It must be there as a necessary ingredient for your own Ascension. Trust that the very movement of the discord and turmoil actually opens the codes of remembrance within you...birthing your Cosmic DNA, your vision of mission and your courage for complete transformation.

When ushering in a new paradigm from a new dimension, everything will begin to feel and look different. Utilize this experience as confirmation that you are entering the unknown expanse of new realities. You have brought templates of remembrance to help guide you in this incarnation. Simply trust that the discomfort of the new terrain is a manifestation of the Ascension process. In any case, you will have to push through the gravity of your current Earth reality. *Reframing your own discord and unease as medicinal wizardry will bring to light that which has previously been impervious and unmovable. The dense debris will rise to the surface, dissolving in the lightness of your "breakthrough" consciousness.*

So, just where are you headed in this Ascension journey? Let me tell you...the 3D world in which you live is very small in its comparison to the many levels, realms and dimensions of the Multiverse. Make no mistake, however, as the Third Dimension is a crucial segment of this ever-living, sacred Entirety of Energetic Realities.

Come with me into the hugeness of these cosmological phenomena. The journey is so beautiful, for it holds what you have come here to anchor on Earth. You, in your higher/cosmic self, have longed for this since you came to Earth. It is time for the Breakthrough! The first step is holding the frequency-knowledge experience of dimensional understanding. I say, frequency-knowledge experience because the most important thing to understand about dimensions is that they are frequencies. Often, humans look at dimensions as if they are places and times; however, it must be remembered (and you have these memories!) that time and space only exist in your Third Dimension. *When experiencing the Fourth and Fifth Dimensions, you do not travel to a new space or time but rather shift frequencies.* All dimensions surround you and are within you. *Your consciousness is the crucial aspect to dimensional travel, as your consciousness is your "signature frequency." Only within this vibratory field are you able to begin to feel and experience other "signature frequencies."* As Consciousness increases its light quotient, it can begin to see and feel higher frequencies. Love is one of the lightest frequencies on your planet. As your heart feels high love, your consciousness or awareness dances with that frequency and becomes that love. Your heart is such a beautiful guide into these higher frequency realms, as it holds the feeling experience of joy, love, peace, patience and beauty. As your body begins to feel these vibratory fields, consciousness holds this awareness and becomes a container for these experiences. That is why we often say, *"Your heart is your best guide to the Ascended Process!"*

So for many, the frequency barometer is set at the human-domain level; therefore, it is calibrated to take the temperature reading of the frequencies in your human/Earth world. It often gets caught in these frequency dances, where breath becomes labored and weighted in movement. This is a dualistic place, so there are polarized frequencies of every kind; as such, polarized frequencies produce half-vibrations not whole. It is in the experience of the 5D that only the *wholeness frequency* can be realized. Time and space are in the 3D and manifest fields of separation. As you feel separate, you spend much of your time and space seeking that long-forgotten union of self and other and Source. The Fourth Dimension is the collision of these disparate, separated pieces, so that they may deliquesce and liquefy into the boiling "soup" of unrecognizable parts. As confusing, destabilizing and unknown as this may sound, the good news is this propels the Now into experience more than ever and the colliding particles of dualism are gasping their last breath. Chaos is the sign of polarizations coming into the middle space of time in colossal collisions of material force… time and space sliding together so that the NOW is an experience more readily available. The Fifth Dimension is where Unity Consciousness can be found and felt.

One of the greatest things that keeps you trapped in the 3D reality is that you have lived this life in a frequency framework that holds the premise that the Universe is contained within the world in which you live! In other words, you have utilized your human paradigm to shape what you believe is true, and so your vision became diminished and your memory of greater worlds became blurred. Getting out of this slumbered state of being is not an easy process, but I am telling you… it is truly magnificent to bring your Cosmic Perceptual Modalities back into focus so that you may see into the invisible worlds of dimensional Ascension. Freedom awaits you and as this manifests, Mission becomes clearer and joyful.

What a dilemma…to have to find your way to what appears invisible, thereby leaving the visible. Is this not why you are afraid of death? For it appears that the event after death is in the unknown, unseen, imperceptible world of spirit. You feel like the only way to know this amazingly lighted spirited world is to experience death. Are you not surprised that you are so resistant to knowing more about this? It has always felt that to know this unseeable, unviewable, obscured and veiled world would mean death. I am telling you, it actually means LIFE. Life within this life…Ascension is simply expanding into that which is currently not seen or felt. It is about bringing that which is not felt or seen into your incarnate self on this Earth at this time.

Expanding consciousness allows you to feel and know the higher frequencies, which are with you every second but veiled by human living. This does not require death of this incarnate life, rather a dying of sorts of the old paradigms that have prescribed this life. *That is what Ascension is: the ability to stay in an incarnated life while moving in frequencies to a higher level of consciousness.* You are meant to be in this process NOW. How wonderful, how beautiful! Rejoice in this knowing and, as it becomes the truth of your energetic flow of consciousness, you will never be afraid of death again…for you will never have to experience an "incarnate life death" in order to Ascend into the next level of Awareness.

Chapter 4

The Now: Recipe for Ascension

THE FREQUENCY WORLD OF THE FIFTH DIMENSION

First, let's review the fourth dimensional experience, as the careening fields of partitioned realities come crashing into feeling the reality of the NOW. The felt chaos captures your attention, catapulting you into the felt fabric of *the moment,* and this necessitates an awareness shift out of the slumber of time/space constraints. Think of the Fourth Dimension as a decontamination chamber. As the heavier, denser, polarized states shatter and splinter, they eventually dissolve into a pool of wholeness that is no longer distinguishable or separate. When stepping out of the decontamination chamber of the 4D, heavy weights are released and a new dance of vibratory orchestration begins. The awareness of this new frequency state of lightness and wholeness brings consciousness into a more clear and expanded state, thus allowing choices and decisions otherwise unknown and concealed by the denser, restricted paradigm. The desire to move out of the heavier, denser realities of the 3D becomes more felt and experienced. It enhances and "powers up" the dynamic and potent mechanisms of your *free will* to enact Conscious Shifts involving choices and movement. The aspiring passion for wholeness and wellness begins to take charge of metamorphic change and movement.

The Fifth Dimension is where the wholeness frequencies are the reality of being fully conscious. Unity Consciousness is finally felt in a chorus of frequency templates. That which has been experienced as a dualistic state no longer exists. Higher frequencies of love, joy, peace, gratitude and grace are experienced by all. The very core of causal dualism is absent. You no longer have to feel hate to find love, or feel despair to find joy. You are fully enveloped by the frequencies of love and joy. When in those frequencies, anxiety, worry, fear and doubt are soothed right out of existence as they have been held in the soft embrace of these higher vibratory states. The *Paradigm of Resonation* becomes the guiding and all-encompassing principle of vibratory transactions in the 5D. For example, love, joy and peace all have sacredly designed frequency fields that produce echoing vibrations that resound throughout the Universe. Those fields begin to discover, attract and dance with like frequencies, creating the dance of the Sacred Figure 8 that is the fabric of the Fifth Dimension. Imagine that when you feel love, you automatically bring the same frequency back to you, creating a field of wholeness and certainty that is found in Unity Consciousness. No longer does love live in a field of neediness, greed, divisiveness, or even the dense desire for safety. Trust and separation are vague memories of some distant past in the land of 3D living. There is no separation when the dance of the Sacred Figure 8 is totally experienced in the Now, sending pulses into infinity. There is no need to trust when the Law of Resonance is operating, as all things vibrate at the same level as you. Imagine that you are totally aware and conscious of always making choices to keep your own field in these beautiful, magnificent higher states of being. You would do nothing to fall out of grace with these beautiful, formulated, 5D frequencies because it just feels too Magnificent. You will feel that anyone who is there with you in the 5D reality is doing the same and, therefore, the state of trust is no longer relevant! Journeying in the Fifth Dimension is simply a matter of consciously experiencing the moment of NOW and the place of HERE, the highest frequencies that reverberate within you, gently waltzing with the Universal Law of Resonance.

*The Fifth Dimension is a place where everything is frequency in the dance of the Universe and time is simply the totality of being this experience...*space and time becoming one in the All of Everything. The most stunning thing about the Fifth Dimension is that individual consciousness is never lost, all the while feeling the Pool of Infinite Oneness...beautiful and magnificent. You might say there is only one duality, the soul consciousness of you and Source, that is within the infinite domain of All That Is. One unique, sacredly designed you that is birthed to experience and reawaken the creative Source Spark within, thus expanding your consciousness into the higher realms of Ascension frequencies. In this beauteous motion of sacred activation, you, through your soul-gifted free will, choose to expand this inner sanctum of wholly/holy experience into the many worlds surrounding you. In so doing, you join the chorus of the Sacred Song of Source Flow into infinity to make conscious the movement between Creator and created. What a Mission you have! Peaked your interest?

Some sweet notes for your soul yearnings. Let's discover how your soul might unfurl these wings of song. As you experience the vibrations emanating from these pages of written words, you will begin to feel *"the what and where"* dissolve into the timeless place of *felt frequency;* and so too will the *"how"* move beyond prescriptions into the ever-flowing frequency experience of fifth dimensional realities.

1. OPENING TO THE FREQUENCY PARADIGM

The "how" begins with the most preeminent and sovereign of prescriptive Ascension channels. If you follow this particular road, you will skip past all other suggestive processes, saving time and space, by simply "being" the Being present in the spaciousness of the Fifth Dimension. This is the most important process of "how" to bring Ascension into the Earth realm. *Everything is frequency in the dance of the Universe.*

As you read the vibratory codes within these pages, you will come to experience the unfolding of the You who has come to Earth to bridge gaps that are found in the plummeted unconscious realms. These gaps are responsible for all feelings of alienation, separation and smallness. As you allow yourself to become a vibratory connoisseur by the very act of reading these pages, you will experience the expanded frequencies in the multidimensional realms around you. In doing so, you are completing one of the most important missions of this incarnated life: bringing these cosmic energetic fields into the Earth realm. In the ardent study to become an Ascension Light Warrior, you solidify and anchor these frequencies on the Earth plane. You produce the "step down effect," whereby the phenomenon of cosmic consciousness and Ascension can be examined and explored in your fields of science and metaphysics. This creates the new Cosmic Science of Consciousness and transforms your planet and the Cosmos forever. You are the bridge-makers by the very act of your experience. You see this is the bridge, as the experience itself is the magnet pulling in and mending the gaps so that the grid of all can be seen and felt by more and more humans on the planet. This happens on an individual basis and only then can it transpire globally and cosmically. As you begin to feel the rising 5D pulsations, they become more tangible and measurable to the New Science Minds and the New Human Hearts. You are a frequency antenna that calls in the language of the multidimensional Universe. By stepping this into the human experiential domain, you bring this expansive, transformative occurrence to the whole planet and all her inhabitants.

As you dive more into the esoteric, intangible senses, it should be known that you become more of a magnetic force, attracting the higher realms of Ascended Vibratory Fields from farther and wider reaches of the Universe. You have this power…you are that magnificent! Remember, the tangible, visible data streams are already within your sphere of 3D understanding. By definition they already exist, producing frequencies that shower you every day with old data racks of past frameworks and formulations. Now you have been given a task to pull data from long slipstreams of consciousness grid fields from other multidimensional planes. It is your higher conscious self that has been ready for this! There is a huge opening right now from the Cosmic Time Grid, sending tremendous light streams of Ascended Travel. Don't try to decipher this book or any invisible experience with your 3D mind. Allow it to surround you with the movement of sound vibration, as if higher Source Light is raining upon you. As you gather the universal codes, essences and grids of light information, these ribbons of information to Earth are brought in producing a *step in* of more decipherable information for everyone else. Make sense? Be careful; don't make sense...*be the sense*!

Remember, you are a deciphering device as you elucidate the higher realms in language for humans through your experience. As you *language* your experience in sound, movement, words, colors and sacred design, you are a cosmic translator. No easy task, but ah, what a wonderful experiencer you will become!

2. THE 3D QUAGMIRE: HABITS ARE HARD TO BREAK

It is most essential to understand how the pull of the 3D gravitational field impacts you. There are so many programs derived from human living that have been installed into your thinking field and the idea of who you are. Many of these structures in which you live give you the illusion that you are safe and secure. Yet, how could this be when you live in such an unsafe, sometimes harsh and inhumane, world that the human species has raced to create! It is a time to break free from old habits of thinking, feeling and being that often keep you in the "static cling" of 3D debris and dross. Often I hear your battle cry, "Yes, but by what methods or means do I use to dissolve the old paradigm?" I say to you, "The most important means is the act of Conscious Commitment to the spiraling movement of soul transcendence as you utilize free will to make this sacred choice to join the Ascension Channels of Change." Say a resounding, yes... right now...and know that the very action of this cherished covenant begins to resonate with the higher frequencies of dimensional mechanics, thereby quickening and strengthening the process of this most magnificent Metamorphic Event.

There are pragmatic steps to take as you hold this "habit breaking" commitment and begin to release yourself from the heavy densities of 3D living. It requires being *awake* and *aware* of the triggers of old patterns, shifting the will and desire towards new ways of thinking and feeling. Most themes will revolve around safety, separation, alienation and fear. Your system has been wired to survive so when fears, anxieties and old worries surface, these antiquated habit structures are triggered to bring comfort and soothing. There are so many dense soothers provided in your world, which unfortunately keep you mired in old habits of 3D behavior. This behavior often invites, unwittingly, more "frequency triggers" of hide and seek. They hide in cloaked rooms of smallness, all the while seeking asylum from the onslaught of everyday living. For example, the electronic devices of your world do such a disservice to the higher Ascension process, because they keep you captured in the immediacy of relief. If you saw the harm that these instruments cause to your life force, you would opt for the new circuitry of the 5D immediately! While becoming familiar with the idea of an "invisible worldwide web" is a beautiful step towards understanding the Cosmic Web of Light that connects and holds you, it unfortunately feeds your ego more than your spirit. It is indeed another paradox, as you see... your world presents you with so many varied and difficult paradoxes. It is all part of Dualism. At a time when your global world has become so unstable, convoluted, and topsy-turvy, you have an upsurge in electronic technology that keeps you drowning in the impenetrable and opaque world that surrounds you. You become "wired" to this invisible, wild world of immediacy and seek answers to soothe, while solidifying the circuitry of a world in chaos. As you have more ways of receiving incoming information about global uncertainties, it appears you have more technological habits to soothe yourself in the midst of these confusing, unpredictable times. What an illusory figure 8 of 3D co-creation. Interesting, huh? Perhaps a time for a little bit of rewiring! There exists another worldwide web of consciousness waiting for you. Can you be more "well conscious"...in other words, staying awake and aware regarding the frequency diet of mind, body, heart, soul wellness? This creates transparency with yourself about internal motivations for the "what" you are truly searching for in the twists and turns of not only your electronic worlds but the outer world as well. In those moments of complete awareness, you are in a position to make a choice to return to your inner commitment to discover the world of cosmic origins within. Once there, sacred vibrations in this inner sanctum will embrace your soul and hold you in stillness, opening your heart to the truth of YOU. How beautiful!

So what tumbles you into the oblivion of your 3D realities? Are you aware of the triggers that cause restricting reactions to surface within your body, mind and heart? What makes you fret and worry... what causes you to reach for a pacifier...what deep dross lies waiting in your subconscious to connect to old timelines of fear, doubt and the "itty-bitty" you? These are where your diminishment programs persist. Know that these realities have been co-created by you and the history, stories and programs of this particular incarnated life, all creating heavy debris keeping you Earthbound. There is no need to be in those realities to solve them. So many human dramas are rather unsolvable because their overarching purpose is to keep you in the 3D figure 8 of diminutive, dwarfed frequencies of a very small, incarnated life. It is not always this way in the 3D worlds; nevertheless, humans have chosen to live more in the element of shadows, hiding in the eclipsed world of the shrouded self. While there are certainly immense lessons of learning there, it is now time to reap the harvest of such umbrage, illuminating the lighted way. This does not have to be your reality anymore, because your mission is to break free of this limited understanding of YOU and come to know your Magnificence!

Pause long enough to know your triggers and programs that are human 3D bound. Stay aware of the states of being that let you know they are saturating you. It is most difficult to move away from something that feels so familiar it simply blends with the very fabric of who you think you are. As a result, you simply lose consciousness of such things. Know the difference between those states of being and the deeper you within. Remember, the architecture of this incarnate personality is only the structure you are currently housed in. It can feel so intimate that you can't distinguish yourself from these material forms and concepts of you. Know they are insoluble and, therefore, not the problems to remedy. You are here to move into higher states of consciousness. After all, that is what you have carried so tenderly and ardently to Earth. It is yours to simply **Be** this.

3. LETTING GO OF TIMELINES

Timelines are the pathways that hold many of the descriptive and prescriptive recipes for living and dying. Releasing depleted and infertile timelines is crucial, not only to free yourself of their burdensome agendas but also pivotal to learning to jump towards higher parallel lives (more on parallel lives later). There are many destiny paths in one incarnated life. Many factors are part of this, including free will, synchronicities and universal principals. At every choice point, you have free will to embrace one life path or another. Your choices will resonate with where you are on the continuum of your consciousness evolution. For instance, if you are motivated by fears of separation and deprivation or doubts about your significance, you will probably choose paths that mirror these frequencies. These paths will then fuel emotions, thoughts and behaviors that match those resonant states. The more you travel particular timelines, the more you become entrenched in those timelines. Soon you won't even recognize that you are the one making decisions as you look upon the people, places and programs in your life and simply act in resonating vibratory states. These timelines hold your ideas and the main components of your personality. They also might hold other incarnate lives that echo similar themes. So you see, when you begin to look at the course of your life and identify particular "destiny paths," you have the opportunity to not only let go of timelines related to this life but, perhaps, other lives you have lived. Some timelines are so familiar that you may think it is simply your destiny to live within them. It is crucial to know you have the power and discernment to not only identify redundant, repeating timelines but to release them as well. If you hold your magnificence and significance in high regard when presented with choice points, you will resonate with those destiny paths that reflect these truths about you. Now we are talking about aligning with the highest, preordained potentiality for this life you are living. I believe you call this Manifestation Laws of Attraction: that which you resonate comes towards you in abundance.

Developing conscious awareness of the tattered road maps that lead you to the denser and sometimes dangerous landscapes of human creation becomes most critical. Truly, some of these panoramic views are quite dramatic, yet you may still become frozen in time as you gaze upon the scene. You can let go of the old guideposts and learn to live in the moment of NOW which allows your deepest heart-wisdom to guide you. When you release the old mapping methods and accept traveling into the unknown, you open the potentialities of universal synchronicities at the same time. As you learn to flow in the potential of new timelines, you open the possibility of creating these timelines with Source sacred flow. Remember, solidified timelines are like deep ruts that cause difficulty for forward movement. Flowing potentialities allow more choice, even if in strange and exotic lands. When your vision is ensconced in the landscapes of old timelines, it is very difficult to see coexisting and more harmonic maps of the Cosmos. As you are able to discard old stories, dramas and paradigm models, you have the opportunity to look around and see the Universe whispering to you with guidance and suggestion. You still are the one "in charge" due to free will; however, instead of the overwhelming push of familiar timelines influencing your decisions, you now can work with a sacred Universe of choice points. The higher you vibrate, the more the synchronistic world opens up to you, and in this you have more options for your consciousness expansion. You can then choose potentialities that might create a larger and more expansive timeline for this life. How beautifully grand and glorious! As you make choices to follow higher missions of consciousness evolution, the Atlas of Ascension becomes more Cosmic, leading you to see your Galactic Hugeness. *Creating a timeline that embraces your highest potentiality births a harmonious song that serenades the world with your deepest Cosmic Self.* When in this kind of creation, you begin to synthesize with Source Energy. Your total light spark within begins to resonate, opening more vision, more expansion, more synchronicities, and more juice for the skyrocketing ride to your High Ascended Mission! The dance of the melodious, cooperative embracement from Source is amazing. Instead of a heads down, shoulders slumped posture found in old timelines, your head is high and mighty…looking at the stars in Oneness.

Old timelines are those pathways that are worn and marred, yet all the while familiar and safe. There may also be wonderful creations birthed en route that you bring to these new timelines. It is important to note that unfolding new road maps is not about new timelines per se, because eventually you will leap from "time" altogether when ascending into the Fifth Dimension. This is the time of Now dancing with Source into infinity. In the 5D, timelines are created every second and never attach to any one destiny path, but instead open to the many and all. Timelines become moments of Now, that never stretch into long hallways of stagnation. Yes, you are capable of this! The more you leave the one and open to the many, the more you are headed to the Oneness of Being…a beautiful paradox indeed. You are neither who you have been nor who others have thought you to be, and you are not the descriptors you have assigned to yourself. You are an ever-moving, ever-undulating, ever-changing Being, dancing with the universal flow within and beyond. This is a most important time on planet Earth, as you have the opportunity to step out of the karmic wheel! You no longer have the weighted past determining the future. What you reaped in the past, or what lessons you have failed to learn, no longer are variables determining the repeating pathways of future incarnations. In other words, the outmoded "handwriting on the wall" no longer dwells in the home of Soul Matrix. The Earth is now receiving tremendous Cosmic Light fuel to enliven your ability to leap out of the karmic wheel of cause and effect. You have come here to be in this mission. As you increase your light quotient of higher fifth dimensional frequencies, you receive the potentiality codes for jumping timelines. No longer are you required to have the repetitive beat of old lessons created new, but rather you become the producer, the co-creator of the upward motion required for new Ascension movement. After all, your mission here is to percolate and spawn new timelines of Ascension Revolution for Earth, rippling this swell of Divine frequencies into the Cosmos. Know that these fertile creations fuel others in remote places in the Universe. Trust this magnificence in you!

4. THE HOLDING POWER OF BELIEFS

So let us tackle some of the stickiness to this letting go process. There is circuitry in your brain, body and heart that holds the programmed ways of living life. Your belief system is at the core of this and, therefore, presents a potentially powerful obstacle. Core beliefs that create entrenched timelines and programs:

1. Existentially, you are separate and alone.
2. This one life is all there is.
3. Source Spirit lives outside of you.
4. Earth is the only inhabited planet in the whole Universe.

Such a small place to live if all were true. Obviously those beliefs, whether held in your religious, educational, family or cultural systems, have not weathered well in bringing your species to the next evolutionary level of growth and transformation. Many on your planet will soon realize that those four beliefs are, in fact, the most dangerous.

The new belief system might look like this:

1. You are not alone and never have been separate.
2. This life is one of many incarnations and parallel lives living within your Soul Matrix.
3. Source Spirit lives within you to be utilized through free will to co-create a new evolutionary timeline.
4. You are not alone in the Universe, but instead live in a Multiverse of All teaming with extraordinary life.

Faith in these new beliefs is simply the confidence and conviction to knock on the door of their preordained realities. Stepping through these thresholds takes courage and sacred desire to experience the phenomenon of these Ascended Beliefs. Many of you already understand this and are making great efforts to lead your lives accordingly. What an amazing difference. Yes?

Let's take a brief look at the amazing apertures of these new paradigm beliefs.

❖   **You are not alone and have never been separate.**

To realize that you are part of the Oneness Grid of all life is a day to celebrate. You have simply come to Earth to lose memory templates of this so that you might, of your own volition, come to know the Source Spark within. *This awakening process brings you back to Unity Consciousness, and every time a being awakens from the amnesic slumber of separateness more Source Spark is created in the Universe.* Isn't it simply grand that you are here to create more firelight in your Galactic Home? You are not only "not alone"; in fact, your biggest, blessed mission is to feel your magnificent self while you bathe in the pool of Oneness Frequencies. In the experience of aloneness as you feel separated from the All, Source Intelligence continues to "see" you as a created one, uniquely designed yet fueled from the Sacred Wholeness. This very "seeing" signals to you, and somewhere in the process of searing separation you journey back home to your Sacred Design. Your desire to discover this truth ignites the heart maps, lighting the home within where deep resonance is felt. How marvelous to see the light within and know it is that light that unites you with the All of Everything!

❖ **This life is one of many incarnations and parallel lives living within your Soul Matrix.**

Many of your religious programs have instigated the belief that this life is the only one to live. What a devastating diminishment program. It is such an omission of the most beautiful veracity of your Soul Matrix. Not only does this keep you fragmented, but also suggests that your soul is quite diminished in its capacity for life. Your Soul Matrix is actually amazingly extraordinary; designing, planning and executing so many lives for you to learn, manifest and create. *Thinking this life is the only one is no different than thinking that life on this planet is the only one.* See how small such thinking is? You have many lives to inspire you and the truth is that, in your many lives, you have created an alchemic recipe for this particular incarnation. I would not be here if this was not so! We will discuss Incarnated Lives later, but for now know that you have many incarnated lives…almost as many lives as you have moments in this particular life!

❖ **Source Spirit lives within you to be utilized through free will to co-create a new evolutionary time.**

There is nothing that is created without the Creator. Think about it… whenever something is birthed, there must be a "birther." We all have opportunities to continue birthing this beautiful, creative dance, and so the Multiverse continues to expand! All living matter and non-matter are Source-driven. To believe that you are separate from Source is one of the greatest myths created by your human programs to diminish and submerge Soul Light. Understand the paradox in this dilemma. As you feel separate, alone and perhaps abandoned by Source Light, you know the darkness that follows. It is often in this darkness that you come to know that which is truly in every cell of your body, for you indeed hold the spark of life source. You wouldn't exist if you didn't. However, free will gives you the choice to stay in the amnesic absence of your Spark Source Light or to realize the truth of why you are alive so that you might come to know your grand mission, especially in this life at this time. Darkness only exists when the light remains in the unconscious recesses of your mind-field. Notice your radiant self is still there, but simply dormant as it waits for you to awaken.

It remains apparent that many humans insist on creating things from a diminished state of being. One understands quickly why dominions of power, domination, divisiveness and separation are born within your world. In that darkness, your magnificence remains obscured and veiled as you create the madness that only dark without light can create. That is your power even without Source. Think of your power with Source!!! It is your free will to decide to be without the light and reject your truest, deepest Soul/Cosmic Self. Don't you see why this time of your Ascension is most marvelous? It is a time when Earth can transmute the darkness and enter the inner light of higher consciousness to create illuminated energy fields beyond your wildest imagination! Ah, what beauty the Ascension journey is, as one dimension dissolves into the higher domains generating a light burst of "fire-force" frequency fields expanding into the Oneness of All That Is.

❖ **You are not alone in the Universe but instead live in a Multiverse of All teaming with extraordinary life.**

To limit understanding of life forms in the restrictive space of your own planet is to hold hostage your deliverance to your own true magnificence. As beautiful as the biodiversity is on Earth, life in the Universe is so extraordinary, boundless, complex and amazingly elaborate. *It is not surprising that your own demolishing and death-defying ways of limiting life, even on your own planet, would set a pace within your consciousness that would diminish the prospect of teaming life elsewhere.* As you begin to honor and cherish life on planet Earth, a code or pod of information will open that will help you remember the truth of life that abounds in your galaxy. Everything is frequency!!! *So as you treat your own life and that of other living inhabitants on your planet with sanctity and reverence, you will create a tremorous vibration that will shake open the knowledge and wisdom of life in all other times and places.* As you revere and celebrate life, a frequency within is created that begins to merge with the Life Force itself. In this coalescing fusion of life frequencies, you come closer to all life around you from the below to the above. Look into the heavens on a dark night to see the bright lights of star bodies and feel the pulse of your being move to the rhythm of their heartbeats. Feel this connective labyrinth of life and you will know that we exist, not only "out there" but also here on Earth. I have come so that you might know this. Every word on these pages echoes that truth. Can you feel it? Isn't it so much fun and exciting to welcome and begin to imagine the many life forms? In so doing, you expand your own field of light and love. How wonderful. Yes? You will learn that there is no wasted space in the sacred grid of the Universe, but only wasted time! Space is filled with life moving in the Ascension Grid towards Source. It is all happening Now. No life is less or more valuable than any other but simply moving at different speeds and motions with differing quotients of waking/sleeping, all with the created Source Spark within. When we all participate in this eloquent and stirring celestial promenade, we expand the Universe with burgeoning particles of love and light. Care to go on this ride?

5. FREQUENCY DIETS FOR THE NEW CIRCUITRY

Living in this new paradigm takes tremendous fearlessness and fortitude both for the new circuitry that has to develop and the weaving of such new thinking and feeling into what appears to be a 3D world. Everyone on the planet is going through "frequency shifts"...some knowingly and some not. Either way, it is pretty topsy-turvy to feel the rearrangement in body, heart and mind.

The Body: Home of the Soul Temple

Let's start with the body of you, for the body often goes through apparent changes as it becomes lighter in matter in the physical domain. As you actively participate in these transformations, by changing your "frequency diet" you will feel shifts more acutely. As a result, your body may feel a bit disturbed during this turbulence. As you withdraw from addictive, denser patterns of body treatment, it is not always a smooth process! It is important to begin to look at how you fuel your body, as you have become so comfortable with physical habits that you might have forgotten how dense your "nourishing regimens" are. I am not just talking about the nutrients of food intake, but also the awareness you have for what the body needs. Think, for instance, of the various addictions prevalent on your planet and it becomes clear you have lost touch with your "sacred body." In fact, it is often the body that suffers most from your amnesic soul state. In looking for soothers to numb the agitation that comes from the fugue state of diminishment, the material body is often abused with the very soothers that eventually endanger it. The human culture is clever in that it has produced things that can numb rather than awaken you. It should be noted that Earth itself has a plethora of vibratory states that are there for your awakening! However, in your wish to survive and have power over your environment, you have produced such dampening effects on life itself. Even food sources are diminished in their capacity to wake you out of body slumber! So, it is a crucial time to pay close attention to how you nourish your material body. As you treat your own body with more sacred sentience, only then will you be able to treat the body of your planet with sacred awareness. *As you feel the steady life vibrations increasing within the material plane of your own body, you will align and resonate more intimately with the sacred life pulses of your planet body.*

Ah, so it follows. As you raise your own light quotient in your body, you make possible the Earth's transitory crossing into the higher planes of Ascension. Quite extraordinary...yes? Perhaps you have not realized that feeding yourself into wellness not only saves your planet but also catapults her to the Fifth Dimension! Hopefully, this is a wonderful motivation to take a look at the frequency diet of your physical being. Can you begin to distinguish what is light-driven versus dark-binding? You have numbed your material body with such dense things as smoking, drugging, drinking, sexing, and much more. It has become so anesthetized and out of focus that you have both learned to tolerate these states and forgotten what it feels like to be *running physically in the light matrix*. Your body has the potential to be in total alignment with the world of lighted expansion; however, it also seems capable of tolerating considerable abuse and waste. It is amazing to us that you can so easily abuse your bodies and not know the difference, until you become sick and tired. And even then, it appears so easy to deny that which made you sick and tired. You wait for body recovery and soon return to old patterns, ladened with dense energies. We understand that the body is where many of you seek shelter, as it can bring pleasures and soothing experiences. It is time to develop that wonderful subtle discernment that says, "What soothing feeds my higher light quotient or what pleasures bring an amnesic shade over my consciousness?"

One of the hallmarks of fifth dimensional reality is to feel the ecstasy aroused from the lighted consciousness within material form. The beautiful experience of the lighter body accelerates portal openings or receptor sites to house the higher cosmic energies coming into the Earth at this time. Bringing your body into optimal light functioning is critical for the Ascension process. As you begin to feel the frequency templates of the 5D, you will be astounded by your expanded abilities to heal all that is within you and even that which is around you. It is quite a wonder to have the capacity to heal that which ails you, that which is out of balance and that which does not serve you. You have all this creative potential lying within the quantum body…waiting for the release of all old paradigms of the maladies of wholeness so that your own creative source matrix can bring you to a new sense of health, wellness and the completeness of the lighted way.

Of course, one place to start is what you actually choose as food for your body. There are many foods on your planet that have become contaminated and tainted by chemical and environmental compounds. Just as you are exposed to environmental hazards which dim your light, so too has much of the food line become murky and dulled. There is a perpetual downward spiral on Earth at the present time, from the very seeds you plant to the finished product on your eating tables. We understand how difficult it is to "eat well" on your planet now, especially in light of quick and easy access to what you call "fast food." You have developed so many ways to quickly satiate appetites and satisfy hungry cravings while leaving others on your planet in total starvation mode, without food or cognizance of their hunger. Perhaps some of you covet food so that you might forget those that have none. Remember, your planet is in a "dualistic framework" and so some of you will sit on opposite sides of the continuum of hunger…some holding a constant hunger state while others experience a constant satiation state. A good way to avoid global hunger is to deny it exists in you. This is how polarization keeps itself alive and well. If you never have to hold the opposite, or even acknowledge its existence, you keep the divide wide and far. With global connections through various mediums of communication, there is not only an awareness of starving populations of numerous inhabitants, but the realization of a dwindling healthy food and water supply in what you call "developed countries." Yet, bringing "wellness foods" to the All on your planet seems a distant reality. This is not to admonish you, but rather awaken you to the forces that feed the physical human so that you might make the "transformative shift" towards the lightened body of you. Again, as you treat sacred your own physical form, and as you feel the lightness of being seep into your material world, it will be impossible to refuse others the same. You will want to feel the beautiful *Figure 8 of Resonance* as you look upon your fellow Earth dwellers. You'll be inspired to resolve, renew and rejoice in your planetary wellness paradigms. *A most marvelous and magical result of Ascension movement is that your own light-fueled experience begins to create a passionate appetite and thirst for the All to experience, thus creating a reverberating state of frequency exchange. The One will inspire and fuel the All and, in turn, the All will create resounding templates that encircle and galvanize this new state of being…thus creating the resonant Figure 8 of Oneness once again.* In this way, you will be assured that you can hold the new timelines in place within and beyond. You will, however, be doing much weaving between paradigms in the beginning of this "lighted wellness movement." Do not look upon these weavings as failures, but rather the necessary movement to form the skyward pathways to the new vistas of consciousness!

As many of you are aware, the "diet craze" on the Earth plane has provided the opportunity to understand this weaving phenomenon. You often swing from the restrictive adherence, to supposed diet foods, to your voracious appetites of ravenous desires run amok. Too restrictive or too rapacious are just opposite poles of the feeding dilemma. Staying on the side of either is simply dense-inducing madness. *You have lost the art of "body listening, body reaffirming and body lightening" artistry skills.*

+ Body Listening: the ability to know what you need by simply listening to the whispers of the material world of the body vehicle.
+ Body Reaffirming: the ability to take action towards such whispering notes, increasing the voice of the body towards rapturous and resounding directives and desires.
+ Body Lightening: the ability to move into the lambent and lucent frequencies of the ascended buoyancy of spirited matter in physical form.

Body Listening

It is so important that you understand there will not be prescriptions or panaceas for feeding your body here. You have had plenty of "food specialty regimens" and expert opinions in what or how to nourish the body. The trouble actually begins there, as it denies the voice from within. You have so easily taken the position of the "unknower" that you have forgotten how to listen to the "knower" within. It is so interesting that you have bypassed your own material world even though you have so ardently searched for external answers and direction for this very material world. Would you not ask a crying child what they are feeling? Or have you ever wished your dog could speak, so you might know what ails them? Do you not look at your natural world for clues to see what it might tell you about the environment? I believe you have dog, horse and tree whisperers that are able to "listen" to the inner stirrings of these beings. Yet, you do not seek the beautiful wisdom that comes from "listening" to your own inner "biosphere." Knowing how to feed your body is, therefore, not about content but the process of listening, thereby knowing the directive signals for the journey of Ascension Awareness.

You have the conscious ability to know not only what your entire body needs but the specific components as well, whether organs, cells, DNA or life circuitry. Begin simply pausing before creating a meal to become aware of your body, and then ask it. It is not so much that your body won't speak, rather it is that you have turned down the volume of its voice and so do not hear the faint whispers. If you heard the voice speak, there is much you would simply not eat! Can you feel when it is drowning in drenched confections and numbing refreshments? So first, it is most important to establish a "listening practice" every time you eat…before, during and after. Be conscious with your body. Clear your "eating tables" so that you might have room to focus on the body exercising with foods and nutrients. You can't be an observer of what you eat if you are watching something else while you eat! You are the expert because you live within the walls of your material self.

Many ET civilizations do not find it necessary to have experts tell the inhabitants how to fuel their physical fields because they have never lost their body consciousness. Thus, they have developed the healing mastery of their own bodies. What a beautiful wonder! It is how some illuminated worlds have achieved such longevity and well-beingness among their species. Know that you have given your power away and always, when power is given away, you lose parts and parcels of your consciousness field. You can bring your awareness back into the lighted way of "well body." *Listen to the faint stanzas of muted notes and you will hear the various refrains of future body requisites for light transformation.* If you develop skills of "body harkening," you will begin to feel the difference between an orange and a cookie, or the green life food and the brown stiffened food. It is not so much that you need to deprive yourself from the delight of the cookie, but when you understand the difference of want your body will assimilate accordingly. Committing to this listening process is the start to bringing lighter frequencies into the domain of the material world. The body knows the difference… it is the alive place of the life pulse. Bringing consciousness to this knowing is the key. At first, you may only receive sketchy direction, but follow it and keep listening. You will soon know the broader and deeper strokes of the artistic mosaic of your material world.

This body listening, of course, also applies to soothing elements you bring to your body beyond nutritional entrees for sustenance. Can you listen when your body screams for rest and relaxation? Do you even recognize the signs and cues for needed pausing and deep breathing? Do you know when your body home needs touch, embracement and healing enhancements? The body is actually a wonderful guide for lengthening life and enlivening your Source Spark. This is especially important for *this incarnation*, as you are here for such a magnificent and momentous Cosmic Mission! Can you listen to the callings within that might lead to the drinking in of the sounds, sights, touches and tastes that quiet and rejuvenate the body? Can you tell the difference between those and the ones that rattle and jolt the body into the dimming valleys of flat tones and colorless scenes? It is most beautiful to listen to the "elan vital" humming frequency within, so that you might identify those things that enliven and magnify the body's life force. This *conscious listening*, in and of itself, can stir forgotten memories of the expansive soul terrains, igniting dormant DNA codes for healing, longevity and cosmic expansion. You may ask, "but what shall I listen for?" If I told you the song to listen for, it would be my song not yours. The task is to have patience in the hearing of the body song...for it is yours and yours alone, unique in the Source Field of All That Is! Listen carefully, for only you can hear it and only you can follow the Pied Piper who glistens with the physical matrix of you. When you begin to hear the notes of your sacred design, they will spring forth to join the chorus of all voices who dare to express what they have heard!

Body Reaffirming

Even if you begin to "hear" your body's material song, the tricky part for the human species is to bring this explicit listening into the fruited action of animated movement. Listening produces the opening, the dance of the inner world of sacred form with your consciousness. Following the strands where the whispers lead is the movement towards creating the new circuitry. You might say this is the changing of the guard from the old paradigm of the diminishing body to the new revitalized material world of you. Even when you begin to hear the body voices within, your old patterns of "frequency diets" are hard to break. Given the choice between the orange and cookie...you may even hear a hushed tone that says, "peel the orange" all the while you are already eating the cookie! It takes great awareness to realize that one of your most powerful diminishment programs is that found in the urgency frequency of immediate gratification! But before we dismiss these quickening needs for "filling up," it is important to note that perhaps there is something mysteriously compelling, deeper and momentous in theses urgent whispers. A calling for something more, something more abundant, something more abundantly nourishing, something more abundantly nourishing for the awakening within. Listen carefully and you may hear the rumblings of these newly discovered appetites that are uncovering not covering, expanding not contracting, enlivening not numbing. ♡

There are many entrenched human paradigms that block this affirmation process. The fear of separation and abandonment has worked its way into your food chain. The story on the surface is that satiation from the outer world will shroud the bedeviled agenda of the old paradigm that you are not enough. So you search your world to discover what you can consume to make yourself feel abundant and safe. There is another famine within…the neglecting of the deep truth of your "enoughness," your grandness, your magnificence. Your soul appetite awaits you and it is a most interesting place to discover where your deep hunger lies. As you take action in the new body wellness paradigm, you begin to clear the channels to be able to feel, hear and see your deeper yearnings. When the physical realm is clear, calm and settled, you have more access to higher consciousness and transcendent experiences.

It will take curiosity and motivation to begin the journey of changing patterns. As you take action towards the lightness of your physical being, you reaffirm your mission as a Light Warrior activist! Listen to whispers of the "body wisdom" and let your active response be the manifestation of this in your physical form and in the world. Following the threads of body wellness affirms your commitment to the task of manifesting the "soul-quest" to your higher consciousness.

So today, can you engage in one "body affirming behavior" and pause to feel the after-effects? Can you be an aficionado of frequency detection? Perhaps you won't feel the subtle realms of body mechanics, in other words you might not feel the delight of the orange traveling in your internal material world and the cell life reveling in its delight. However, you can simply taste the frequency of the orange and pause to experience what that is. This is actually the fun part…the gift of consciously choosing resonant frequency diets for your physical home. There are so many options for this beautiful journey. Let your body wisdom speak through all of your sensory modalities. Think of your senses as portals to the material world of you. What guests would you have coming through these passageways? What frequencies do you wish to have roaming the hallways of your home? Are they ones that move about with tumultuous and disturbing vibes, creating pandemonium in the cell life of your body matrix, or those that move with grace and light, transfixing your cells to dance in ecstatic revere? You might want to choose the latter, if you plan to be in the tempo of Ascension energies. Be aware and conscious of what you choose today. Take action to reaffirm your deeper soul mission by treating your material world with sacred choice and manifested realities. Be curious how long you can stay awake in the new paradigm of body mechanics living in the light.

Body Lightening

There are so many beautiful gifts for enhancing and expanding the light quotient in your body. This is all part of remembering and embracing your journey to experience *conscious connection to the All of Everything.* Always utilizing your own consciousness to hold the whole of everything, you begin to design pathways and choices that actively guide instead of passively move through the halls of the old paradigm. There are three areas to master in this world of bodily mosaics: what you deliver to your body, what you tell your body and how you interact with the external world.

First, let's explore the lightness that you "import" to the inner world of your body. As you come to know and are acutely aware of the incoming frequencies and how your body holds them, it is easier to move towards the higher vibrations in nutrients, movement, touch, sound, sight, taste, etc. As you feel the effects of different internal experiences within your body home, you will be able to discern those things that feel buoyant and those that feel more dense. It becomes easier to gravitate towards those things that leave a lighter footprint within the chambers of your physical world. This allows you to experience the movement of inner body lightness and joy. The amazing thing about Ascension is that as you increase the light quotient, your sensory modalities change as well. You will feel as if someone turned up the dials of all of your sensations. Your toleration for heavier, denser input will decrease as you experience its devastating effects and anesthetizing influence. Lighter input will feel more astounding, full and tremendously energizing. You may find you taste, touch, smell, see and hear in a broader and deeper spectrum of frequencies. When not ladened with heavier sediment, your body begins to feel its ability for optimal functioning, opening to an aliveness never before experienced. This "body renaissance" then holds the possibility for higher consciousness to expand, enlivening the Sacred Figure 8 of body, mind, heart synchronistic flow. Now the most material part of you can embrace this ever-evolving world of ascending movement. As your body can hold this, it will be able to hold the transcendent movement into the 5D without having to perish. Not a bad motivation…yes? *Remember: this is a most breathtaking time, as you have the amazing and most astounding opportunity to Ascend to another dimension without leaving this particular incarnation.* So you see, bringing high consciousness to the body is most important…don't you think?

Second, what messages reverberate from your mind and heart regarding the physical world? It becomes most crucial to consciously alter the dialogue between body, heart and mind so that messages of beauty, safety, wellness, healing and flawless functioning are abundantly circulating throughout the network of this tangible, material fabric. As you affect the material world with your higher conscious choices of thought and feeling, you enact one of the prime principles of the Ascension process: *As Above, So Below.* Consciousness is your main portal for the rising potential in this incarnation. As you acknowledge the power of your Cosmic Consciousness, you bring in the spiraling light from the transcendent realms and, in doing so, activate the potentialities lying await within your incarnated body, heart and mind. Changing the "message boards" of your inner world is crucial. Make sure the handwriting on the walls of your "incarnated body" is penned with the lightness of being and the sureness of your Ascension mission. Practice creating new scripts for the paradigm shift into the

Fifth Dimension! Can you begin to imagine the soundings from the inner dialogue of the fifth dimensional You?

Third, moving your body in the world to create the waltz of you and all that surrounds you now becomes possible! In what time and space does your body reside? Allowing the body to step with nature is especially crucial at this time because your Earth is ahead of you in the Ascension process. The frequency quotient of your natural world is lighter and filled with more fifth dimensional energy emanating from each new plant, mineral and animal being birthed. Placing your body in spaces that are of higher frequency ratios can be most medicinal for soothing and healing. Feeling the vibrations from the natural world allows a resonation and directional flow towards the Ascended, lighted pathways. When unimpeded by human carnage and demolition, the Earth is an extraordinary planet. After all, she is a most magnificent, light-infused Celestial Being who has offered herself to this planetary incarnation for the mission of traversing the fifth dimensional realms. Feel her, be with her and tend to her as if you are the gardener of her most luscious body. Dance with her vibratory tessellations of the lightness of her being. Feel the Sun of her sky protector warming your skin, and the Moon of the moving waters lighting the dark contours of your consciousness. Allow the wind to whisper mysteries made clear, and the stillness of the night embrace the *spaces in between* the textures of the embodied self. Let the smell of fresh dew moisten the brows of your closed eyes and the scent of roses arouse the memory of temples frequented in dream visions. Get to know the gifts she gives, drinking them in with the full gusto of rising oceans and howling wolves. Then take this "renewable energy" and bring service to her needs and desires, creating the spiral of love that has no receiver or giver but simply the oneness of resonating frequencies…to and fro… movement with stillness…all at once. The Earth is perhaps your greatest teacher of love and the lightness of being, and in this you spiral into the multidimensional world of All That Is. So, take time to rock and roll with the dance of her spirited motion. You will begin to hear the echoes of the Divine symphony, transforming your body into a cosmic craft for this metamorphic journey. ♡

There are so many choices of body co-mingling on Earth. Choosing to mix with other humans is a big one. As you are certainly aware of the negative dances you engage in with other humans, it is essential to become conscious of choosing to be with those vibrating entities who emanate a strong life pulse of light. Be aware of the bodies you choose to bed with, work with and play with. As you discover other "light activists" on your planet, you will be amazed at the fueling process that happens as you co-create with them. It is the resonation of vibratory states that expand your light quotient in its potency. Allowing yourself to be in the spaces and times where light body activation can occur is paramount. Look upon your world and find the "temples" where high consciousness dwells. When these spaces are unavailable, utilize the amazing place of your imagination to create them and allow your body to be restored by the sweetness of the Temple rhythms.

Once again, inundate this bodied incarnation with choices that embrace the magnitude of high consciousness. Intend to choose and manifest the dance of illumination and your body will rejoice in the vertical rise of soaring movement. The listening, reaffirming and lightening are yours to choose. The specifics of those choices create the arena where free will comes alive in the most 5D sense and divines those manifested action moments towards the Ascension journey. *Remember always, to be in the motion of grace and beauty, and to bring service to that which moved you into lighted action in the first place, creates the sacred loop of reciprocity.*

The Heart: The Singer's Song

The heart is the barometer for the "whole" of this incarnation. It has great capacity for creating such beautiful euphonious melodies of love and joy. Yet, it also can house the edgy, dramatic and sometimes bewitching winds of emotional hocus-pocus, blowing fiercely and breaking eardrums when coming too close. The heart is a gatekeeper of all things done wrong, holding and sometimes hiding fluctuating feeling states that are often hard to dissolve. But, oh, how the heart is the holding power for sublime rising states of high frequency. The heart is the sacred tool of the Divine Feminine, loving with fierceness and gentleness all at once. *The heart is the sanctified passageway from which all transformative frequency templates can be experienced to catapult one into the metaphoric process of Ascension.*

It becomes paramount to the Ascension process to dissolve dense, compressed feelings that hold the heart in captivity, that keep you tethered to timelines that have long ago lost their luster. You have perpetuated the idea that you have to *resolve* old hurts, dramas and historical places of trauma. Unfortunately, this belief causes constant consternation as you review that which you think needs resolution. This only grips you in the dominion of old 3D timelines that burden the soul and consequently fuels and encases your "incarnated personality." Spending an inordinate amount of time on the players, places and times where these formulations take place, you inadvertently solidify yet abandon the "feeling frequencies" that are produced in the first place. When you reenact injustices and heart hardships in your mind's eye, you become convinced that solutions lie in the outside world. When you peel away the players, places and times, you can access the vibratory fields of "feeling states" that need your attention. Most denser human feeling states originate from separation themes and old, self-diminishing paradigms. You see, your hurt, torn and tattered self has always been looking for love and healing. After all, if love and healing had happened in conjunction with the important "causal" states (people, places, times and incidents) you would not be carrying them in your satchel of grievances. They would no longer be influential in the narration of your psyche, stories and history. Yet, humans in their present state can be so reticent to solve problems with sacred love and high peace. As a result, many deep injuries stay in the corridors of self-description and explanation, all the while shrinking the memory of the most Magnificent Self. The specifics of the hurtful heart form bastilles for keeping the pain held captive, but the walls of the locked up heart are no match for the venerated High-Heart frequencies. Once surrounded, the facade of false screens dissolve and the leap to freedom can be felt within the whole of your incarnation. The expansion of you becomes swiftly accelerated...in fact, you might not even recognize this new state of being! Past events become less important than the liberating, spiraling experience of love. So, if you strip these deprived feeling states of externalized logistics (stories, people, places and times), you are simply left with emotional frequencies that are in need of love, caring and compassion. *The good news is that you, and only you, have the medicinal hermetics for such an alchemic journey of healing and revelational transformation.* You have the capability of "frequency-jumping" to the illuminated vibratory levels of love and light, and creating energetic fields of high frequencies...showering, easing and dissolving that which has been left behind.

Take one incident that has happened to you recently and find the deepest, emotional state triggered. Do not concentrate on externally perceived specifics, for they only have the power of the 3D world. Begin to really *allow* these vibratory "feeling states" to be felt and curiously *embrace* them, in their purest form, without the mind's commentary. After this immersion into sacred acceptance, vision enveloping them in the healing sanctity of your compassion, the lightness of love and grace. Allow them to absorb this remedial and sanative heart remedy slowly and assuredly, and feel the dissolving of the externalized incidents. Once healed, there is no need to hang on to that which held them in the place of injury! Do not let doubt or dismay cloud your "tuning in" to this most powerful process. Remember, you will not find the solution in a world that is a step behind you. You are a consciousness Light Warrior, learning to utilize fifth dimensional, High-Heart frequency fields! The sights and sounds of some event simply create the sheets upon which the music is written...change the music and the sheets disappear, no longer cluttering your library of songs with old tunes that no longer inspire.

When this happens, that which produced the hurt vanishes into the world of light. ♡

It is time for the realization that your heart can produce "timeline jumping" by its capacity to embrace the *human* you in softness and grace. As you practice this with specific "heart incidents," you will become more adept at "timeline jumping" into the cosmic orbits of parallel lives, incarnations and even with dimensional realms! (more on that later)

So, this is quite an area of mastery. It may initially look like you are discovering the keys to freeing yourself from the gravitational pull of the densely designed, emotional province of 3D living. What a wonder to know this may just be a practice ground for the fifth dimensional skill of "timeline jumping." *Nothing is what it seems, but everything is a clue.* It is important to remember that dense feeling states have the amazing capacity to keep body and mind tremendously busy. In the archives of a life lived, there are so many attachments to events, stories and historical dramas. These inner ruminations create the contours of your personality and all that you believe is true about you. This often keeps you captive within the world of this particular incarnation. It is these dense, opaque, frequency-feeling states that provide the fuel to keep the aged stories burning and the binding of your personality intact. In generating a new harmonious song, you can create the exalted chorus that is in rapture with the grandest part of you. This, in turn, ushers in the genesis of the "higher consciousness" that knows and remembers the cosmic truth of you and creates the momentous rippling of you into the Sacred Figure 8 of All That Is. What echoing notes would you like to feel in the corridors of your heart? Remember, You are the master composer!

The heart is one of the greatest gifts of the human species. When freed of the darkness, it has a direct line to Divine Source frequencies. After all, love is the fuel of the universal flow and so when the heart sings the poetic notes of love, the entire Universe listens. *The heart creates the buoyancy by which the Ascension journey can be held in the stillness of illuminated movement.* Exhilarated, heightened, vibrational fields held in your heart begin to pulsate and flow outward, calling for resonant fields of High-Heart frequencies. The more bounteous energetic fields will begin to attract you and pull you closer. The law of 5D manifestation will come into fruition as you find yourself in swirling fields of higher vibrations. Resonant energies will fuel further your High-Heart wisdom, power and strength to create *As Above, So Below.* Synchronicities will abound, at first appearing as pinpricks of hope and jubilee. Soon you may find yourself living in a world where every turn is connected to Source Light and every breath is in realization of Unity abundance. In this total synchronistic world, the soul dances in the showers of fifth dimensional frequencies.

As you vibrate anew, calling in resonant realities, you begin to sail in the Golden Figure 8 of High-Heart 5D energies. The heart is quite magnificent as it has the capability to hold these higher-dimensional frequencies of love, joy and jubilation, creating a beacon not only for other humans to follow but extraterrestrial and celestial planet Beings as well. When the human heart swells into this action, a signal is produced that tells the story of Earth readiness as she accelerates her charge into the Fifth Dimension. At that time, assistance from the multidimensional realms and extraterrestrial civilizations will be astounding. *As Above, So Below* will take on a whole new meaning on the planet.

Allow this to be motivation to breathe in compassion and joy. Let your heart fill with the high frequencies of beauteous bounties of unity and love. Your heart was meant for this. Can you feel the new cosmic song sung by your heart? Can you hear the rhythms shift, sending waves of magnificence into the Universe? Whenever you lose your way in the myriad of mazes on the Earth plane, listen carefully to the newly laid notes of the soul's voice beating softly in your heart. ♡

On your Earth plane, it is currently known in your sciences that the heart carries frequencies far out into your world. You call them electromagnetic frequencies and have discovered that the High-Heart vibrations have longer and smoother lengths of expansion, while the more dense, edgy feelings have short and chaotic frequency patterns. Makes sense…yes? Thank goodness! Otherwise you would be receiving a lot of dense, vibratory fields from every corner of the Earth! You will discover that there are other frequencies as well emanating from the heart. You might call them cosmic/soul resounding pulses from your heart chakra. This is one reason why prayer, meditation and spiritual belief patterns can be healing to the surrounding world. As you intend to send the matrix of love and light healing to one or more, or your whole planet, that act creates an inducement field for the receiver. The power of this is dependent on the receiver's openings and the giver's clarity of High-Heart manifestation. In giving, if you have not cleared your heart of lower vibrational feeling states, they indeed may hamper the power and strength of the energetic field you are sending. Think of it this way. As you send out higher vibrations that are surrounded by lower energies, the wavelength may only be able to travel so far. As you are clearer and less ladened with such heaviness, you have the power to send these fields to the Moon and back if you wish. So you see, lower frequency fields you house in your heart (jealousy, diminishment, anger, hate, for example) hamper and diminish your ability to heal and love with your heart. It is like having a beautiful cup of pure water and when it spills it seems to spread everywhere; fill the water with mud and heavy debris and it only affects that which is closest to the cup when spilled. This same holds true for your own healing capacities. You actually have come with the ability to not only heal and serve others and your planet, but yourself as well. Remember, this power can only be unveiled once you have cleared your heart residence of your unwieldy, burdensome 3D detritus. As your heart begins to spin with illuminated light frequencies, you will discover the amazing power of love to revive, regenerate and invigorate this process of transformation. However, it is so important to realize the astonishing, dampening affects of doubt and disbelief. For if you wish to send prayers of illuminated love and healing to the world, make sure you do not shroud this with the oppressive weight of old paradigm thinking and feeling. We see how humans "half hope" that the power of sacred love and cosmic light can actually transform and uplift the world. As a result, they send half-streams of tightly wrapped, hopeful messages, wondering all the while why they don't have a grand effect. As you clear your own heart field, you allow the natural potency of the cosmic heart to unfurl and spring to life. This is the most powerful energy on Earth! The frequency of Source Love, consciously felt and then given, heals and inspirits both you and all those receiving such gifts. The Sacred Figure 8 once again appears and imprints on the world of 3D Earth. Can you imagine communities of awake and ascending humans sending these Source pulses of light and love to the whole of Earth? Oh, what miracles and magic you would see!

It should be noted that the receiver of such glorified soul-treasures always has the action of free will. It is one of the universal laws…nothing can be forced onto another without their ability to be instructed by the domain of their free will. Unfortunately, many humans have violated that law. Nevertheless, especially when it comes to these higher principles of the heart, one thing that is crucial is the openness by which one receives these gifts. You might say, "Who wouldn't want to receive the High-Heart frequencies?" However, you do not know what another soul's intention and mission is for this particular life. This is very complicated but suffice it to say, what is most important is that you stay in the complex mission of *your* life, Now.

Know that what you give may not always be received in its entirety. Perhaps, someone does not heal or some Earth crisis does not subside after your beautiful High-Heart mission work. Do not utilize this as proof that this does not work. That is your little mind working overtime in a dualistic paradigm. You cannot know what is in the highest good for someone else; however, the act of being in the High-Heart is more far-reaching than you can even imagine. You might also want to choose to open your receptor sites for such cosmic love to come to you. I think you would be surprised how many beings of all kinds are sending you this rippling, elevated, 5D frequency field. Open and you shall receive; in so doing, you make room for more lighted illumination in your heart. This begins to feel so amazing and incredible that you naturally gravitate to these states, even after spending some time in human fields of dynamic overload.

Let me briefly summarize this most important Ascension journey of the heart. I have heard humans say, "What is this thing about light and love? Isn't it just something to say when things get tough?" I say, "It is not something to say, it is something you have yet to learn to really be." As you become more conscious of those lower/slower/denser heart feelings, you can begin to practice dissolvements in the midst of heart incidents. As you utilize the beautiful, soul song to bring notes of enchantment and bliss to the heart chakra, you will feel the lightness of love and compassion creating a buoyancy never before felt. This in turn resonates and calls in aligned 5D frequency states, which serve to increase your abundance and flowing, vibratory heart states. The Sacred Figure 8 of *As Above, So Below* comes into fruition in the heart arena and you are carried to higher levels of mastery. The fabric of the synchronistic Universe opens for you to see and know with more depth and breadth. This enables you to utilize this wondrous dance to service your planet and all who inhabit it, which of course includes you! The healing powers of this 5D frequency grid are most magnificent. When freed from the heaviness of the 3D plane, you will be able to soar to great heights with new alchemic processes of magical potions. Coming into great service to your planet is one of the stepping-stones in Ascension transitioning. You will be able to send High-Heart frequency grids anywhere, anytime, transforming the very planet on which you live. This is the truth of your powers. You can become part of the healing domain, traveling with vibrations at distances farther than the end of the rainbow!

The Mind: The New Circuitry of Ascension

All programs and historical data get stored and filed in the circuitry of your mind field. Your mind field is, of course, inclusive of your brain but also expands into the quantum world of electromagnetic energy created by both your physical brain and consciousness. *Consciousness is the energetic domain contained in this particular incarnated material field, together with your Soul Matrix vibratory field.* It is held within a bio-mathematical, material field of each particular incarnation. You might say consciousness fields are the frequencies emanating from the voice of soul. As the sounding from the soul steps down into physical form, it becomes narrowed and compressed. As awareness becomes more focused on the particular incarnated material life, the outer rings of soul sounding become more eclipsed. When you come in a physical body, the consciousness frequency is dimmed down; as you awaken, portals open to bring in more of your high frequency consciousness. Higher consciousness is that which is always with you in all incarnations and holds the awareness realization that this is but one life. Bringing higher consciousness into this life is part of the Ascension Mission at this time. Your mind circuitry is made up of both actual neuro-circuits in the brain and frequency corridors of your consciousness field. Cosmic Consciousness integrates the circuits and pathways from your heart, mind and body together with your soul overlay, and is the mainstay for the creations of all that you are. As your cosmic awareness increases, you begin to feel and experience the higher-self frequencies. This, in turn, allows the potentialities from the higher realms to manifest the Ascension realities, riding the slipstream of soul consciousness incarnating on Earth, at this time and in this space. The beautiful metamorphic transfiguration of the colors, sounds and sacred designs of Universal Oneness are arriving in the plane of your current incarnation. How extraordinary!

Breaking Old Connections, Building New Circuitry

According to your science, you have over 100 trillion neural connections in just your brain. Quite a bit, wouldn't you say? You have already determined some of these connections simply through habits and thinking patterns formed from the experience of this human incarnate life. There are so many more beautiful energy, neural networks yet to be created in the hallways of the material world of your brain and mind field. Imagine that in the electromagnetic quantum world there are even more gateways to the ***infinite consciousness network*** of Unity Source Intelligence. Some habits are potentiated towards this and others towards the material plane of human living. One must be very careful what patterns of behaving you want to reinforce. As you begin to live by resounding patterns of the neurocircuitry of the material world, the portals for higher consciousness dim and close. Keep in mind that the neural networks that currently make up your brain are from past experiences and knowledge. It is far too easy to be content with the way in which you have learned to think and know the "truth." If you take the same old pathways, you solidify the old paradigms, including what has been known up until this very moment. By definition, you are then thinking in the past. The most frequented path, then, is the most readily available for options of understanding, thinking, solving and resolving. As a result, recognizing patterns of thinking is crucial, as most incoming information is categorized in your old library system. When you process information, it tends to seek out the most closely matched frequency pathway, often the one most utilized. It finds some kind of match or resonance within and speeds down that sensory corridor, bolstering its power to become the road most traveled. These habits of your brain are not easy to break. It is not unlike the route you travel everyday to go to work or the food market. You don't have to "think" about it, as it is a very utilized pathway in your brain. Habits and behaviors easily determine brain circuitry, and this brain circuitry then determines habits and behaviors. Soon you may have an enclosed system of thought patterns and, therefore, **predetermined** behavior from dimly lit antiquated hallways of electrified, if not petrified, material wiring. Sometimes it is quite curious to us that you can find life-sustaining energy with such an enclosed, partitioned-off system.

BUILDING FIFTH DIMENSIONAL CIRCUITRY

Expanding the Range of Potentialities of Awareness

The act of awareness creates an expanded frequency range magnifying the lighted pathways towards Conscious Awakening. It would appear that so many things you do and think are from the unconscious mapping of some past paradigm, stagnate of new life force or new lighted energy. By the very act of opening and becoming aware of the frequencies of consciousness in every thought, feeling and action, you open windows allowing the breath of the Great Life Force to fuel and expand your world. Simply allowing your "awareness state" within to take the lead brings the *awakening conscious self* to the forefront. You might pause to ask:

+ As I am awake in this moment, what vibratory state is felt in my body?
+ As I am aware of my heart essence, what movement becomes apparent?
+ As I pause in this awareness, can I feel the frequency of stillness begin?

Allowing new frequency patterns to emerge in conscious perception creates beautiful, expanding circuitry to hold the within and the beyond. Remember, everything is frequency so it is important that you bring awareness to the various sources of the vibrational fields within you. Thoughts, feelings and actions all create expanding vibrational fields, not only impacting your own perceptions of existence but the sentience of all others as well. Your thoughts, in particular, are huge dictators of your reality. Yet so much of your reality is conceived from the unconscious realm and, therefore, is generated from that which already exists in the libraries of past matrixes. Consequently, you have minimal creative power to shape and spawn new realities. In addition, the sense of self becomes more materialized and less connected to the soul wisdom of your higher consciousness. Habits and patterns continue to be formed by the physical, sensory perceptions that are often stuck in a wheel of materialized forms and concepts. Portals to higher, nonmaterial realities are often dimly lit and more difficult to find. Becoming more consciously aware is like turning on a light in the dimmed hallways of the field frequencies of the All that you are; therefore, becoming mindful of every thought and every action is critical. At first, this may seem impossible as you enjoy the assuredness and confidence of the fixed and rooted pathways that you so easily travel upon in somewhat comatose states, half asleep/half awake, daydreaming of what's next or what just passed. As a result, the reality of the Now moment slips away along with the potentialities of expanding portals.

Humans often ask for a book of tricks and recipes for this Consciousness Journey, as if there is some magic treasure chest full of wands and staffs transporting one to the new realities of conscious living. Oh, these treasures exist for sure, but if you are not awake and aware you will soon forget to seek them. Simply staying aware of *where you are* will open the channels to *who you are*. You have been benumbed to the world of frequency awareness in favor of the enticing world of material solidity. Your old circuitry so easily diminishes this Self Awareness. Without *self-aware consciousness*, all power is defused and relinquished to old paradigms of lost vision and hearing. Take your power back; bring your creative potential to this most vibrant moment of all...Now. Are you here now? Can you feel the frequencies jumping off the page, calling you to feel your most vibrant life force within? Your steady experience of the Consciousness Field within and surrounding you expands your world exponentially with depth and breadth. Pause...feel it...be it. ♡

Every time you *become* the experience of this *vibratory field of consciousness*, you create the new circuitry of Ascension within your mind field. These advanced, integrated circuits of the New Paradigm of Conscious Awareness sanctify your journey of discovery and circumnavigation of the Higher Consciousness Realms. How long can you stay aware and awake? What places, situations, people trigger your slumbering self? Can you be more aware of the old circuitry and the triggers that become on-ramps to old and tired responses of your material body? Can you stay alert when you land in old reflections in the mirrors of past realities? Stay curious, stay awake and join the genesis of your own Consciousness Evolution into the invigorating frequencies of the New Paradigm of Ascension.

You now have the capability to produce corridors bridging the material mind network with the surrounding frequency fields connecting consciousness to Universal Source Intelligence. Simply wake up each day with the Mantra, "I am the new circuitry I create." As you say, so you are. The very act of activating the throat chakra to sound aloud the intention creates new circuitry! Remember, *nothing is as it seems, but everything is a clue*. If you think it seems that you live in the reality of the outer world, you are probably beginning to leave your higher mind field. You can generate phenomenon from the universal field of alive, sacred frequencies rather from the material world of fixed, vibrational energy. If you are reading this, you probably do this more than you know!

Meditation

Meditation is the most illuminated opportunity to *still* the 3D mind. All fifth dimensional journeying is beyond that point of stillness…for in the stillness, one can begin to feel the movement of circuitry anew. Meditation and meditative moments prepare the material brain for expanding its material networks, opening portals to the amazing world of cosmic consciousness. The 3D hustle and bustle of the human brain is quite overwhelming. Put another way, your brain is the busiest freeway system in the world, careening and colliding with the ever so quickening input from the external world. It receives tremendous amounts of information on a second to second basis and, in the brain's attempt to make sense of the world, it has become enormously fragmented and splintered. Meditation is a wonderful antidote to the frantic pace of 3D mind circuits. Allowing rest supports rejuvenation, which in turn generates cosmic revelation. It is the frequency experience within those absolute calm, quiet and serene moments that potentiates the opening of cosmic portals to the vistas of invisible, multidimensional worlds. The stillness of the meditative mind allows the expansion of advanced circuitry necessary for the *state of being of the New Human.* Mastering the "still mind" potentiates the opening of sacred portals to the vast and infinite expanse of the invisible worlds beyond. Meditation also inspires chakra alignment and the enlivenment of the Merkaba light field surrounding you. As the third eye becomes enlivened, the frequencies of Source connection and dimensional vision increase. All of this is within the quiet mind field of you! Simply pause...breathe...and be still. This creates the fertile ground for material calm, circuitry expansion and cosmic magnification.

Dreaming, Imagination & Visioning

It is time to take back the dynamic endowments you have been bestowed with to create new realities and visions. You are your own co-creator and so you can dream new realities into being. If you knew how many realities your dreams have already manifested, you would spend most of your time *dreaming consciously!* Take time for an Imagination Practice; dream and visualize the New Realities of Fifth Dimensional Living. Remember, a dream that creates the Sacred Figure 8 of service and love has incredible potency for accelerated manifestation.

The new thinking modalities of visioning, dreaming and imagining, along with the cosmic wisdom channels, are found in that in-between place of brain and mind field. The more novel circuitry you create, the more you will become familiar with the Cosmic Maps of the future that will come alive in the now. Traversing down the hallways of dreamtime and imaginative places requires faith, belief, desire and, finally, the grand *experience* of such endeavors. The only reason you think you can't dream reality is because you have become too responsive and addicted to the realities in the external world that you already created. Unfortunately, when you only spend imperceptible time imagining, dreaming and manifesting, it is easily negated by the stupor produced by your external third dimensional world.

Vision, imagine and dream of the new paradigms to come. Take back your power to be the *embodied soul architect* so that you are no longer at the whim of a material world (once built by you). You have created an outside reality that has taken the seat of dictating and holding prisoner your own consciousness. The external material world is only but a wisp of truth with little life fuel or soul force. You have created a world to hold you that is now devoid of the magnificence of who you *really* are. Perhaps, this is a perfectly sacred design created by you after all. *For as the outside world falls apart, losing its rapture and grandeur and no longer reflecting the magnitude of you, some whisper within arouses and stirs, portending the coming age of humans ascending into soul consciousness, beyond time and beyond form.* This invigorated cosmic consciousness, then, visions and dreams the new lands upon which you will build the New Human Paradigm. It is probably hard to imagine that you have been the creator all along, but perhaps now you can hold the fire of desire to create anew once again. Imagination is simply the experience of consciousness traveling de novo. It becomes the bridge between the neuro-electromagnetic worlds and the cosmic consciousness realms. Sleep dreaming and awake visioning creates this new circuitry, opening channels to the multidimensional worlds beyond. Even when you explore some new pursuit in your material world, you expand the tracts and twirls of your mind circuitry.

Imagination is the corridor by which all other dimensions can be realized. While you are not evolved enough to actually create something out of nothing, you are evolved enough to create grand recipes from the existing synchronistic cosmic frequencies of your Universe. Imagine if everything you dream and vision really exists. It is just that you have learned to travel in the material world and have yet to make journeys in the world of dreamtime as *a felt experience of tangible truth.* As you increase your light frequency quotient, your ability to dream reality will be greatly augmented and amplified. Your ability to vision, dream and imagine will stream the fuel of liquid light into the new circuitry of expanded consciousness. Infusing the contours of space and time with the frequencies of Now catapults you into 5D awareness and the vibratory experience of the ever-expanding moment of *now creation.* You create with each breath of awareness...fueling the new tessellations of higher dimensional energy grids.

Your thoughts create frequencies that have the power to create the realities of tomorrow by simply being free to roam about the rooms of your consciousness home. Spend more time visioning and broadcasting these new inner realities rather than passively reading the news on the scrolls of your social networks. Build the new cosmic networks of soul imagining and you will soon find yourself riding down corridors of creations beyond your current imagination, awareness and fantasy. Once you begin to imagine these realities, you will have the delight of being in the experience. This experience, itself, steadies and embraces the frequencies of the "higher mind circuitry."

As you experience, you become a frequency antenna, a cosmic receiver station, a "sky wire" of incoming dimensional light. You bring in these amazing new realities, not only for your own circuitry but to transform the morphogenic consciousness fields on Earth! If just one human can do this, imagine what a group or community of human beings can do! Dreaming and visioning together has the potential to create exponentially larger fields of vibrational templates, making them more available to larger groups of humans on your planet. This accelerates and expands Dreaming Reality at breathtaking velocities. The most powerful services you can provide for your planet are gathering and journeying with other human cosmonauts who are able to coalesce the visions of the New Earth and multidimensional realms. *Visioning and Imagining are the brushstrokes of consciousness on the sacred life canvas, creating the panoramic vistas of Earth Ascending.*

Curiosity Run Wild

Be curious! To live with inquisitive passion inspires you to peer longingly into the possibilities of the new circuitry. To vibrate at the level of open wonder, and vibrant thirst for that which lies in the unknown recesses of your Universe, resonates with the passageways towards fifth dimensional realities. Thus, the very act of curiosity creates a frequency slipstream that carries you like a starlit craft to mysterious vistas, untouched by human hands. This is one of the most important trajectories upon which you can travel. Even in your Earth world, there is so much to be curious about. The diversity of life itself should occupy you for many a day. How much do you really know about the riveted gaze in a whale's eye? Have you ever felt the beauty a wolf beholds standing on the precipice of mountain peaks? Can you experience the unwavering commitment of ants to the communal goals of food and home? Have you felt the underground web of life that lies in the rooted wisdom of the medley and multeity of the tree kingdom? Have you spent time looking up at night into the cosmic heavens to feel the awe-inspiring experience of the expansiveness of your galactic home? Have you communed with your cosmic neighbors, telling stories of your commitment to soar in the stars in peace and harmony? There is so much to know and experience with the living inhabitants that dwell upon your planet, let alone in the star-seeded Cosmos. Each being is an incredible piece of the puzzle to the mosaic of life on your planet and beyond. Expand your knowledge base and you will breathe new life into the pathways of your spirited heart. The very frequency of curiosity creates portals beyond your imagination. It is a magnet that draws the Universe ever so close, waking that which is within and beyond. Stay curious as you read these pages so that you might allow your channels of experience to swell and surge with overflowing codes of remembrance!

The World of Creative Art

You have so many beautifully inspired artists on your planet. This creative expression is surely connected to the Web of All Creation. It is the spirit that dances through the material human form, creating music, paintings, sculptures and all beauty in art forms and materials. Humans have a fascinating, and sometimes haunting, desire to allow the whispering soul to paint on the walls of ancient caves and sing in the valleys of sacred temples. It is the heart craft that carries these frequencies, expanding the circuitries of body and mind. It is the most universal language you have on your Earth planet. You can gaze at a beautiful painting and feel the heart of the artist without sharing one word of common language. You might say that an artistic creation is a telepathic form of communication. This telepathic "language" creates circulating orbits of the cosmic language of light, within and among. Creative art displays the beauty and truth of Human Consciousness. Journey to a museum, art gallery, sculpture garden, room of dance or music concert and feel the experience enlivening the very core of your being. You cannot behold something that is not already within. You are the music, the art, the movement, the notes. This is your sacred design. It is time to open these channels of divine origin and let your own vibrating, creative zones expand your sensory modalities into the Cosmos, all the while never leaving the world within.

Nature

Experiencing the natural wonders of your beautiful planet is the swiftest way to take flight into the new ascended circuitry. *Nature is the Earth's breath in action.* There are no blocks or obstacles in the naturally vibrating web of life that can be found in Nature. She is already spun with the lighted filaments of Divine illumination and, therefore, every experience is Source inspired. Earth, even with her burdens that humans have constructed, is connected with all of her inhabitants and her place in the Cosmos. Unfortunately, there are places on Earth where there have been tragic efforts at destroying her sacred gridlines of body and spirit. However, even in the zones of diminution, there are still Earth consciousness and frequency channels to the All that surrounds and is within her. In nature you can experience this higher vibratory field, stimulating remembrance and truth of the circulating "light life force" within. Walk in nature with Awakeness and experience the vibrating pulses of the hallowed breath bestowed in material form. Nature is the organic roto-rooter for clearing out clogged human circuitry. If you are disconnected from your Earth and all that she holds, you are certainly headed for a "heart stop," as it surely indicates a sluggish system of pulsating debris. Connecting with your natural world stimulates the higher consciousness experience. The High-Heart vibratory field found in nature is enormously inspirational fuel for building the "brain bridge" to even more expansive landscapes of the invisible realms. Nature holds the sacred path towards unfurling those mysteries of the Universe. Your planet is imbued with sacred designs of enormous magnitude, from the infinitesimal to the grandest. The feminine Nature of your planet is the master Oracle of your material plane, revealing many codes and keys that will point the way for understanding how the Cosmos works, speaks, plays and creates. She sings rhythms and reveals sacred patterns that are inherent in the very fabric of the Cosmos. Can you hear her, feel her, breathe her? Enjoy.

Building the Perimeters for Unwanted Realities

It is important to revisit the somewhat fragile yet beautifully forming state of your New Mind Field. As stated before, your mind field holds and stores all previous programs of diminishment. You have remained within these constrictive walls of thinking to find safety and refuge. You are *now* beginning to come out of the caves of unconsciousness into the light of the day. When doing so, expect old programs and timeworn circuitry to keep its tight hold on how you construct reality. As you move into these mystical and magical worlds beyond and within, it is most vital that you protect yourself. The newly forming circuitry is delicate and fracturable in its early stages. Eventually, as you solidify the network of 5D frequencies, it will begin to embrace and surround you with a calm, tranquil sanctuary that you have never before experienced. However, in the early stages, you may have to close the perimeters of your world to limit bombardment of the often sticky, denser particles from the external 3D world. It is imperative that you understand and accept the reality that this incoming data wreaks havoc on your new, higher-vibrational networks. In addition, these 3D compilations often solidify the old, dissolving neural pathways in your brain…for like attracts like. It is the Law of Resonance. You have become so accustomed to the onslaught of this incoming data stream that, in its midst, you no longer recognize frequencies of diminishing dissonance that are ignited and fueled. If you listen carefully to the uneven rhythms created within, you would soon become aware of that which produced them. This "realized awareness" is then capable of creating blockades, preventing the influx of unwanted material that is overloading old systems of wiring. Instead of learning to repair the infrastructure of your material mind, you might be more inclined to build a brand new energetic field of transporting new ideals, new experiences and new formats for Awareness beyond the material plane. Remember, you are creating a new network within that can house and attract information from the unknown, invisible realms of Source Intelligence. As a result, you might have to completely rearrange your life, creating choice points of where you go, whom you go with and what you invite into your home.

It is most crucial to understand and digest that your electronic devices are mainly there to support the old circuitry. They may deliver information faster than a speeding bullet, but the effect is to shatter your internal world just the same. Much of the electronic revolution is now utilized to create mazes of diminished, vibrational templates that dull consciousness and drain self-sovereignty. Thus, you have given power to these outside deliveries of reality. Become the conductor of modern devices so they may assist you, not bind you. Be watchful and pause in between for longer and longer periods of time. The best they have done is help you understand the potentiality of a worldwide web of connecting grids that lay the foundation for new explorations, curious pursuits and a global sense of the human race. However, as you give up your seat as the conductor, you may be bombarded with fear, confusion, derision and disharmony. Your very dependence on these thermionic devices limits your own telepathic, extrasensory channels for creating the worldwide web of connection...for it is the very fabric of organic material, your incarnate self, that learns to take flight in the ethers.

Can you take a look at your addictions and attachments to this electronic information age in such a way that you can begin to create perimeters to block out the stimuli that feed them? Be careful of that which you think expands your knowledge. This incoming traffic often restricts your spiritedness as it breaches your heart field, bringing fear, loss and hopelessness to the fabric of your being. The old circuitry has quite an appetite to remain intact and unscathed. Yet, in the end, it is exactly that inertia which will take life force away in one breath. I will say to you many times...*your Awakening is that crucial and pivotal to this Earth Ascension.* Know this and begin creating a safe space for the expansion and amplification of your higher consciousness network of beautiful, light-inspired frequencies. This will change the nature of Earth's trajectory into the New Paradigm of consciousness evolution. Design and shape a temple of residence that allows space for the new circuitry to grow and multiply so you might see, hear, taste and touch that which has been invisible. It is a most exciting, yet critical, time to formulate and forge this breathtaking and stunning fifth dimensional reality so that it can be felt, experienced and anchored. As you live this, the ripples begin ever so softly to swirl into the Land of Earth and the Cosmos. You will be amazed and astonished as you become an integral, conscious, living and breathing part of this illuminated cosmic network of etheric worlds. You see, you are not just expanding your own life circuits of sacred consciousness but, in the very expression of such expansion, you are joining and solidifying the Cosmic Web on Earth. In so doing, you have created an amazing service for the Ascension journey of your entire species and those beyond. Breathing consciously within the Sacred Cosmic Design allows the creation of a template for your beautiful human species so that they may join the rapture of the All while, at the same moment, feel the One that you have all come to be! What a truly magnificent Sacred Figure 8!

Spirit: The Dancer of Dreams and The Rebel from Beyond

Stop for one moment and realize You Are Alive! Humans have quickly forgotten this one most beautiful and indispensable experience...your aliveness. As you have become planed and diminished by human living, your awareness of "live" frequencies has been obscured and shrouded. It is hard to hear the call of the sacred wind within, when taking labored breaths in clouded and deserted landscapes of the dispirit soul. Unfortunately, the distraction of time/space paradigms relegates inspirited journeying into the mists of background noise, creating undifferentiated notes of discordant tuning. Therefore, the very experience that keeps you alive resides in the dimmer, obtuse subconscious and sometimes wholly unconscious networks of you. An incredible paradox...yes? To be alive in material form with the consciousness of Source Spirit is the most idyllic and resounding actuality of the human potential. This veneration of awareness then creates the ripples towards the crossing point of the time/space continuum to the event horizon of Unity Consciousness. It is only you that can bring this Source Spark to your worlds. This light fuel is through you and surrounds you in all material forms in your world. This is why you can never be separate because you are Life Source Force and are connected, by definition, to all Source frequencies. Think about it...everything in your Universe is filled with Life Source Force.

In your human incarnate domain of time/space, it is all too easy to conceptualize only in phenomenal, corporeal and, therefore, tangible ways. In so doing, you squeeze the very essence of life force Source right out of you. It is time to bring the beauty and vibrancy of the "live" frequencies back to consciousness. As you do this, you actually fuel consciousness to ride on the wings of Source Breath. It is the "alive" frequencies that connect you, stimulate you and cajole you into spiritual flow and conscious transcendency. You already hold this awareness of radiating and receiving these frequencies, for they whisper in hushed tones to the beat of your heart, and sometimes drum so loudly on the sheathed membranes of your material form that you feel you might faint! Illuminated life force courses through the circuitry of your heartbeat every time the heart speaks freely of love, compassion and kindness. Indeed, seeing the beauty in your world that transmits signatures of amazement and wonder touches and moves your heart into ecstatic dance.

So many things in your world are breathing life force, but your "receivers" for **brio and zest** have become closed or narrowed. The initial external attenuation and curtailment of your vital expression of the fiery, spirited self was probably quite a surprise to many of you in your earliest childhood experiences. Even when born to material form, the "sun" of spirit still dances about with joyous abandonment. Perhaps you can recall a time as a child when your spirit was soaring and you were told, "Enough! Stop!" You began to learn slowly but surely to dampen the sprite of spirit that guided you to the mysterious and magical worlds of wonder and amazement. Eclipsing your lighted force within, you turned on the external guides for decorous fitting and resonant alliance. Your search for that amazing experience of *Sacred Unity while in consciousness* changed as the whispers of the inside world became faint and dulled. When in material form, it is easy to believe that this searing separation from both Source and Individual Spark could be solved by becoming more *of* the outside material world and less *merged* with this beauteous, rambunctious world of spirit. Again, such a strange and difficult paradox: the very uniqueness of you vibrates with *flow life force* that brings you home to the harmonious symphony of All and yet, as you diminish your own distinct strings of musical designs, you leave the soul (sole) instrument in the corners of rooms…unspent, unplayed and unheard. In this place of deafness, where cosmic sounds of the Universal Harp are silenced, you desperately search outwardly for remembrance of inclusion and affinity, thus the external, material callings for feigned unification become louder and more deafening. Soon the human orchestra becomes deplete of the spirited notes of Unity Source Spark, because you (as beings of this material, human world) are the only ones who must carry this vibrational sounding to the symphony of this world. That is why your throat chakra is the most thwarted and diminished of all chakras within your energetic body. As you re-enliven your spirited voice living in the depths of your sacred design, you will release the frequencies that will save your world.

Can you feel the frequencies emanating off this page of worded designs? Let them lighten your spirit and then pause to soar to the depths of your sacred home within, alighting on your wings, taking flight through the Cosmic Windows of your Beautiful Self. ♡

Spiritual teachings and religious traditions often bring a sense of awe and Source awareness to those yearning for soul inspiration and heart opening. However, in so doing, these inroads to a spiritual life often become rigid doctrines of how to live and less of who to be. Often, Divine Source is defined as something that lives in the outer parameters of your life, rather than in the deepest energetic field defining you. Various religious organizations have designed methods and models of old paradigm thinking to block these light-filled, inner pathways to Divine Intelligence, thus creating a paradoxical paradigm. Unfortunately, these rules and guidelines are often strewn with frequencies of control and disempowerment. Frequently the protocols of instruction delineate shunning the very things in life that bring joy, beauty and celebration, as if those very things diminish your connection to the Life Force of Source. What a paradox: to be closer to "God Source" you must rid yourself of your own life God Source Force! The New Human Paradigm rejoices and sings forth: you can be trusted to be conscious of your own divinity that lives within and you will enact the most extraordinary and beautiful fruitions thence forth! The biggest problem with your human species is that you have distanced yourself from this beautiful *Source Energy Matrix* within. Disconnecting from the Fountainhead of All Creative Life Force is surely a destiny path of doom and gloom. You are Source Spark and have been materialized with this Cosmic Life Force to soar in jubilation and magnification of such Divinity. It is time to come back to the truth of who you are and experience this sublime moment when you are in rapture of the embrace of Source Life Force within your own matrix of individual consciousness! This is when Earth shall make her turn into the matrix of love and peace and fifth dimensional Ascension. Know the truth of your own magnificent divinity and flow forth with it into your world. Know you are nothing but Light, nothing but Love, nothing but the Creative Force streaming forth, as you breathe in and out connecting to the ever-present matrix of the Ultimate Fountainhead of Life Force Source! Do you really think, as you allow this to flow within and around you, that you could create anything but Love and Light?

If you ever feel the need to look outward for spiritual guidance and soul referendums, gently walk in the opulence of Mother Nature while carefully listening to the whispering of deeper meanings of Life Force in the oscillating rhythms of Earth. You might even hear the enchanted wizardry of Merlin, spinning tales of Earth, manifesting and teeming with the Magic Spirit in Motion. Perhaps, you are wise enough to walk in the forested grounds at the dusking hours of deep browns and greens, where owls sound the ancient wisdom of lands forgotten. Perhaps you can see the forebearers of your Earthly home, riding the wind in wispy clouds, bringing the dawn of the New Ages to come. And then again, can you sit and breathe in the cherished imprints of Earth Unity that are held in the hearts of your indigenous peoples? Follow the hearted frequencies within, then look around and you will see a world that is simply a reflection of all the wisdom that is you. *Ah, the Sacred Figure 8. All that is you becoming all that is the world and the world becoming all that is you.* How beautiful. How sublime. This, my friends, is spirit life force co-creating worlds with the Jeweled Hand of Source Divinity.

Begin to feel your spirit waltz in the light of the moon, for the moonlight reflects the very light that is within you. Know that when you move in synchronicity with body, heart and mind, you create an orchestra of sounding designs of light that dance with your spirit. Listen to the call back to Source Spirit and feel the bohemian drummer within that quivers with the new pulsations that have yet to be heard on Earth. Discover the tree that springs your heart forward towards the All. Follow the trails of the night sky lights and feel your heart leap with luminous joy. Remember, if you are asking how to take flight in life force, the very question is the weight that keeps you dimly and sluggishly grounded. The mind simply cannot pilot the spirit; instead, the spirit infuses the mind, heart and body. Lead with your felt Life Force and watch all else become infused with the Spark of the Cosmos. Where your Life Force is, there you shall live!

THE TUMULTUOUS RIDE OF THE WEAVE

As you begin the Ascent towards the apex of your evolutionary 5D journey, you will most definitely fall, slip and tumble back into what may feel like the abyss of 3D life. Perhaps, you will take a misstep on some new, albeit slippery, steep slope or simply, in your need for rest, fall into old patterns and habits of safety and knownness. Oh, the grief of spirit to plummet again and again while finding your way home to the lightness of being in your fifth dimensional self. Don't be dismayed for this Sacred Weave, this wobble of sometimes careening and floundering oscillations, is far more purposeful than you know. This Sacred Weave is one of the most important experiences to hold with compassion, grace and deep trust, as this becomes the higher embrace of your "soul knowing" in action. *The Weave is the movement that creates the fuel for Ascension.*

The totality of the Weave, even the brevity of the wobble, creates the aqueous movement that makes that which is stuck more soluble and liquid. As you begin to feel the freedom of this migrational flow, you access a deep natural propellant that moves you towards the light. This is the elixir or golden honey within you that holds the remembrance that you are the resonation of Source Life Force. So, as you experience these new vistas on your dimensional climb, you will experience a burgeoning consciousness that will leave indelible and stirring traces of these expanded horizons, even as you fall into the fog below. The very vibrations created within from these soaring panoramic views will now be trace-memories igniting the fuel to return once again to the ascending process. Each time you experience the Sacred Weave, it will become easier and easier to mobilize these trace clusters of your lighted self. If you do not begin to experience the beauty of you, the magnificence of you, the astounding you, where will you return when you are ready to reunite once again with your destined Ascended Mission?

The "crown" or apex of the Weave, no doubt, can be a bit dizzying, but you will become more adept at consciously recognizing and engaging these lighter, more buoyant, elements of the Ascension process. You may, in your meditative pauses of ecstatic wonder, or your strolls arm in arm with the magic of nature, or healing another with the power of love, be able to gather new light, new laughter, new suppleness of spirit. Ah, to bring such beauty back to Earth to the human domain, where this lightness of being is most needed, is a most blessed and providential soul-fortune! Don't you think? It will no doubt be difficult, arduous and perhaps you will be filled with the heaviness of dismay upon return. As an Ascending One, it is your illuminated task and mission to come with the light, as a gardener might leave the luscious forest with her basket of fragrant flowers and medicinal herbs to walk into the barren lands where blissful aromas and curative potents have not been cultivated and turned into the song of the Heart. I say to you, *you are the bringers of the New Dawn through your **weavings** of Lighted Wings.*

As you bring the "crown-weave illumination" back to your life, you will be able to see more clearly in the glow of this luminosity that which does not serve you. You will develop a keen awareness of sensitivities as you descend and ascend. This may be felt as you dip back into your diminishment programs, and so the corded pulls of the lower realms will be felt more acutely. It may even feel more devastating and desolating as you tumble into the abyss of 3D living, because you have gathered enough light frequencies to see and feel it differently. The Weave is important for it brings more light, but it also brings recognition of what has kept you in the dark. It may even cause you to feel more sensitive, irritable or emotional as the debris fields and the dense trappings of 3D life become more intensely felt. What gave you meaning before may lose its luster in this New Paradigm of Ascending Order. Simply put, you will become more "dark-sensitive." In other words, as you carry more light, that which is still in the dark will become more apparent. Toleration will shift and you may experience this as quite unsettling, as that which you tolerated or even developed an attraction towards in the past may begin to feel disquieting and diminishing. Many events, persons and situations will become less fulfilling, draining the "lighted crown-fuel" right out of you. The unease may push you back towards the behaviors, thoughts and feelings of your old paradigms, just to escape the dissonance created within. In the midst of this, you will now have the trace elements to fuel and "rev up" the high consciousness craft that will propel you back to the vertical, lighted path. Remember, before feeling the ecstasy of the lighted path, you had very little trace lines to follow. You were able to adapt well to your 3D living paradigm, but something in you propelled you to seek that inner sanctum of peace, harmony and love. That, in turn, created the fuel to travel into the enigmatic unknown. The very mysteries of this obscured, yet curious, world created vibrational pathways upon which to return. If you are having a difficult time "slamming" back into your old paradigm of living… congratulations, you are in the Weave! Even as you re-enter this 3D world and your consciousness dims and awareness wanes, please know this truth: you bring curative illumination to that which needs healing and love, therein shaping the New Architecture of the New Paradigm. Each time you take the plunge, you bring new blueprints and advanced codes for the Ascension Transformation on Earth!

When you dip back, know you are not only bringing more light (even if you do not feel that) but you are bringing enhanced illumination to that part of life that kept you hostage and diminished. You must see the world as it is before you are able to create that which it is not. Do not despair as you fall into your dross-filled fields of old, but rather experience this as a gardener's dream where the ground turns into the luminosity and luster of seeds newly planted from the very movement of your ***weaving-lighted-self***. You will then discover the realization of your own deep, inner truth that lies in the whole of you rather than in the remnants of the parts created for this one incarnate self. Unique missions, novel gifts, new essences and neoteric frequencies will emerge from the totality of your Soul Matrix.

One note of caution: do not judge or critique these downward curves of the Weave. Many of the emotions you feel must be followed as they trigger deeper memories of lost times and vanished lives. This can only be revealed by your very humanness. The Human Heart is your best asset during these wobbling times. It is why so many extraterrestrial races are here now. You would be very surprised to know how many in this Universe are intrigued and inspired by the Human Heart. The problem on Earth is that the very beauty of the heart makes it most susceptible to traumas, dramas and heartfelt dilemmas. During these times, the mind overdevelops, closing off channels to the heart; so the heart then becomes numb and sometimes "holy absent." When you are feeling dismayed, upset, sad or angry as you look around, know these are the echoes of your heart. Follow these swelling ripples to the deeper places within you and you will discover the sacred destinies of the human species in vaulted blueprints of sacred design. Perhaps as these memories are awakened, it will create even more "dark-sensitivities," (for example, more ability to feel the truth of global injustices, the disparity of sustaining environments, and the tragedy of lost life, lost species and lost indigenous cultures). You see, this weaving not only opens the vertical ascent into the higher frequency domains, but it also opens your deep-seated wisdom of the beautifully crafted capabilities of the human race. The division between what is and what can be is often so much to bear, but know that as you carry despair, sadness and angst about the human race, you are actually creating the alchemy for birthing the lighted code of heart magic for the human species on your planet.

Somewhere deep within you have a memory of an incarnate life far away on a planet of human beings, where the Ascended process was fueled and directed by the Human Heart. On this planet, the most amazing and beauteous heartstrings sounded the music, like the Pied Piper, for all to follow. There was no destruction of planet or species, as the Indigenous Ones with their Unity Spirit divinely melded with the planet, leading the way, sounding the drumbeat of the Heart Rhythm's guidance. This planet saw no hunger, disease, wars nor division. Only the highest frequencies of the Human Heart were seen and felt throughout the planet. This beautiful human race is moving quickly now, weaving new lands of awe and wonder for the entire Universe of Cosmic Souls. This is one reason your planet, Earth, has created such a stir in the cosmic neighborhood, for everyone is asking, "What happened to the humans on Earth? Where is their understanding of free will and creative choice?" Alas, there is a New Human on Earth now and it is You! Deep within, you have the remembrance of this magnificent human race and this shall guide you in times to come. Know you have gathered a very distinguished audience to witness you in this grand design of Earth Ascension. Can you pause for a moment and feel the curiosity and reverence for the part of you that is awakening in the night? ♡

The ultimate goal of your Ascension journey is to create a smoother, less jolting ride on this preordained Cosmic Weave. While the beginning phases can feel more dualistic in the ups and downs, eventually it becomes a **smoother** ride where you are skimming along in the total, lighted craft of your high consciousness, without pause, without entanglement. Remember, the question is not how to avoid the downward slide or even how to find the way back to the vertical rise, because as you ask this you separate yourself from the very place you wish to return. It is simply keeping the awareness that you are in the motion of the Weave. Imagine creating a lighted craft where you are the one guiding and riding within its center. As you travel and spin throughout the Sacred Weave, the lighted quotient within the craft, while always expanding, remains stable and abundant. Each time you dip down, you not only emanate more and more light from visits to the seat of your high consciousness, you also are more impervious to the "hooks and spears" of the 3D realm. As you become more and more the 5D Lighted One, you glide more easily and with more momentum throughout the Weave. As you ascend towards the "crown of the weave," you create additional quantum portal openings for receiving 5D illumination. As so, it moves on into infinity...*As Above, So Below!* In that smooth, quiver of motion, you become both "human in 3D" transforming all at once to "human in 5D." Somewhere in the middle of this beautiful Figure 8 of weaving movement, you transition to a new domain where curving apertures bring new vistas of unknown proportions of light. This movement of the Figure 8 can be found in every dimension and every place and time. Perhaps, it is becoming clear that embracing this Ascension weave is simply a prelude to journeying in the vast realms of the multidimensional Universe. Somewhere in the middle of the accelerated velocity and exponentiated motion, a portal of stillness opens to the new Ascended Dimension. *Even as you are one unique individual consciousness moving towards Source Oneness, you are* *riding on the Illuminated Dance of the Weave, breathing in the Lighted Path, thus expanding your one consciousness into the Consciousness of the One.*

Chapter 5

The Inspiration of
the Fifth Dimensional World

THE INVISIBLE WORLD

To feel and know the invisible world, or the world of unknown parameters, realms and beings, is the complete antidote to all 3D habits and fears. Yet to enter these new frontiers of fifth dimensional frequencies, you must be fearless and have an utterly undying thirst for the mysterious. As you begin to cross through the gates of the 5D world, you will soon have access to a boundless library of astronomical wisdom. Once and for all you will know with certainty far reaching truths beyond your Earth world. All this can be felt while remaining in this current human embodiment! *This 5D Ascension process does not require an incarnate death, but instead a rebirth of life within a life.* How joyous! The karmic wheel comes to a halt as you begin to experience the vertical rise of the Ascension Path. You are not here to learn from the continued spin of old paradigms, where outmoded and outworn thinking and feeling are the glue for those paradigms to continue to control and diminish. The karmic wheel has provided the circuitry in the past by which you can return to familiar territory to learn new lessons and renewable contours in recognizable terrain. You might say, *you continue to meet that which you have sown into your resonant field as it reverberates back to you for further upgrading and enhancement.*

All of this is important for building a quotient of light potency for this Ascended Incarnation. Now, instead of gathering materials for rising to the ceiling of that particular incarnate lineage, you are on the cosmogonic "Ascension Wheel" breaking through the 3D canopy to a brand-new dimensional plane. During this revelational process you no longer identify your darkness as an opportunity for a redo, spending unnecessary time in denser resonations, but rather it is a time of cultivating the technology of dissolvement and leaping. In other words, you are here to learn anew, transcending old platforms of performance and dancing a new matrix into being. It is a most momentous and astounding time on Earth, where the praxis is experiencing the core of your magnificence, building fuel for surpassing the confines of the horizontal realm of your physical world. As you are released from the gravity of your 3D world and the entrenchment of the karmic wheel, the vertical rise begins and this new "Ascension Wheel" spins the new light of consciousness transformation. As you begin to hold this new lightness of being, you create new "diamond-crystalline" receptor sites within your quantum body to hold the new frequencies of the 5D.

It is a new thought, a newly found freedom that you no longer have to "work through" old issues, dynamics, dramas or traumas but instead boundlessly leap into the higher truths of your magnificence. Up until now it has been conceptually and spiritually easier to think you must simply learn to "do it better or right," so the lessons are learned in this life to create better lives to come. (Since all lives are happening at once, you may want to see it as being able to send light right now to another life right now.) In this very moment of now, how joyous that you have an opportunity of a lifetime to jump slipstreams of old material to new, albeit unknown, lands of "higher" living. You no longer have to ride the karmic wheel to land in another lighter/higher incarnate life later, but rather you have an amazing opportunity to leap to the already new you in this very incarnate life. No more incarnate leaping per se, but instead leaping *within* incarnations. *Learning to surpass old incarnations creates the material of an ascended incarnation, which then holds the ability to leap within incarnations.* This is what ushers in a New Paradigm or Dimension. In order for a new ascended level to be reached, it is crucial that it be created from *within* the incarnate consciousness. It is this very transition of your current incarnation's consciousness that creates the Ascension journey!

THE JOURNEY OF MAGNIFICENCE

There is a tremendous surge of Cosmic Light streaming forth onto your planet now. It has many magnificent, illuminated sacred designs because Earth is perfectly aligned with the center of the Universal Synchronistic Web. This alignment provides the cosmic quantum matter that inspires the alchemic processes necessary for planetary transformation. Remember, as the "one" you are here for the many… so essentially, you are the *au courant architect* for building the foundation that will usher in the New Earth Paradigm. It is, therefore, essential that you become familiar and accustomed to embracing the frequency template of your own inner Magnificence! You see, becoming and "being" the vibration of your true soul magnificence actually creates a frequency matrix by which you can absorb and hold the most intense, brilliant and elegant incoming light of Cosmic Source. The very experience of knowing and being your magnificent, beauteous self actually forms and augments a light template capable of receiving downloads and upgrades from the incoming Ascension Light Grids. If you are in your lower, dimmer sense of self, there simply won't be receiving stations for such Magnificence. Oh yes, the ego may desire to get involved with such magnificent notions of the self, but this Soul Magnificence has little to do with this incarnate version of the egoic self. It stretches far beyond, creating illuminated bridges to the brilliant elegance of your Soul Temple…for this is about the overriding arc of your Soul Matrix coming alive with the light of consciousness within you! Then, the Synchronistic Universe utilizes resonant fields to inspire and boost creation, and so there is a beautiful, magnetic dance between attracted universal pulsations. Everything lives in frequency fields interacting and folding within and around each other, and all are catalysts for repelling or attracting motion. Diminishing, denser energies repel and oppose expanding and lighter frequencies; just as lighter, expanding vibratory fields invite and summon illuminating energies. You might say, there are no receptor sites in the Matrix of Magnificence for diminishing reverberations.

As a Light Warrior, it is a vital prerequisite to utilize the fires of *free will* to see through the clamor and tumult of these raging times and know you are one step away from the absolute Magnificence of who you are. The most important impetus for letting go of old diminishment paradigms is landing in the evolutionary awareness of that which lies deep within the caverns of your higher/cosmic self. As you traverse these transcendent, resplendent and exalted places, be careful…for as you come closer to your lighted self, the old programs of fear and doubt will fiercely surface to keep you at bay. They are simply there to be thawed and liquefied then effervesced into the ethers of transformation. In the past, you have become immune to concern for the ailments of the soul. Stay awake now! Feel the burn and find your Divine Will through the fires of deep knowing.

The discovery and experience of your Magnificence and lighted grace creates a frequency that is crucial for the fuel of your Ascension. You went through an amnesic process upon coming to Earth. Many of you still believe the old programs of disregard, but you no longer need to stay in the deep freeze of negligent and heedless blindness. You can open your soul eyes once again and "See" the brilliance of who you are. You cannot see the magnificent transcendent process of Earth's Ascension until you fully acknowledge your own, surrounding yourself in the actual experiential encounter with your brilliant light frequencies! As your consciousness moves into the boundary-less territory of this experience of brilliance, you open the portals for Universal Divine Source to flow through you, enabling cosmic codes and essences within to open and fruit themselves with the aroma bouquet of new birth. Then and only then will you have the "eyes and ears" of the Heart to fully see the truth of these times. Think and be the impossible in order to discover the imaginable world of your Magnificent Soul Light!

Something quite miraculous happens as you vibrate within your expanded consciousness, your *soul-lit* self. You begin to resonate with the higher frequencies of Magnificence that are all around you, that are waiting for you to be aware of their sweet embrace. Notice how easily the denser material plane pulls at your attentive processes and curtails and dwindles *soul-fire awareness*. As you raise your vibrational quotient of light energy, reverberation with corresponding frequencies will create ribbons of illuminated pathways for connection and merging. This is the building block for dissolving separation and entering the Golden Age of the Figure 8 dance.

As you feel these echoing vibrations, they will emerge from the invisible and make an appearance, magnifying and fueling awareness of your own abundant potentialities. You will come into clearer awareness of the Synchronistic Web of All Life Energies, as synchronicities abound in the wild world of the Source Web. *This is the interconnecting network of all creative light frequencies holding the labyrinth of all life in sacred sync, where everything is entangled, none separate from another, and merged and coalesced by the very force of the Breath of Source.* Walking in this while awake is the material of dreams. Want to begin dreaming? Fifth dimensional frequencies of abundance and healing are always dancing in this Cosmic Web. As you learn to vibrate these **soul-lit** frequencies from within, you create a reverberation with this Cosmic Network, creating the Sacred Figure 8. Resounding frequencies arouse and inspire the process of the Ascension mechanisms of manifested Oneness. Opening consciousness to this enlarges the portal for manifestations to occur. Manifestation, after all, is simply the ability to resonate within with that which surrounds you...one compounding another, coalescing into a slipstream upon which you begin to not only live but soar.

As you become a higher frequency Being, you resonate or message those higher frequencies that surround you, moving those particular strands towards you. Only those universal, coded light ribbons that are needed and desired for your Ascension will come to you. You have a frequency mechanism within that responds to the Ascension process, turning up and lighting certain codes. They, in turn, attract those same vibrations in the lighted Universal Web that surrounds and is within All. As this glistening, lighted fuel enters your within world, it expands the Sacred Truth of who you are. Slowly at first but eventually picking up enormous speed, you begin to live in another reality, which becomes the luminous, textured material of the Fifth Dimension. At first, perhaps, something that was invisible becomes visible or things you would have missed before are birthed into being from this synchronistic Universe that you can now see and feel. You notice these synchronicities everywhere and, in that, you become part of the Golden Figure 8 of Ascension. Eventually in the Sixth Dimension, *you are* of this world of synchronicities, one begetting another, never separate, never passive, rather wholly creative and vibrant in the Web of All That Is. So you might want to get on with this task of being so Magnificent, for you have come with the formulas within for great expansion, breaking through the bondage of human diminishment to the elevated heights of human Ascension. This, my friends, will truly be a magnificent experience of soaring freedom as you take flight from the untethered boundaries of time and space! After all, you agreed to come here to discover your Magnificence once again. And by being this Lighted Self, you will bring the New Dawn to Earth.

Unity Consciousness vs. Separation Paradigms

Your true "holy" essence has been camouflaged while living in the separation paradigm for many a time on Earth. It is true that when soul sparks enter a material-formed incarnate state, cosmic memory is often dimmed and sometimes lost. Awareness and, therefore, conscious experience of the Great Round of Unity Consciousness recedes, thus curtailing the one truth of Unity Oneness. However, do not be dismayed for the Earthly human state of separation provides a great opportunity to experience the seeming paradox that Unity Consciousness can be felt once again, even in the separated suits of material form. There is nothing quite like the fiercely powerful fuel that is created from the searing experience of separation, thus igniting the awakening journey towards Consciousness of Oneness. When consciousness resides and lives in just the "one" (meaning you), it also provides quite a time to explore the processes by which the "one" might finally inform itself of the One. It is important in the process of Ascension that you have a go at total submersion into the incarnate material life. You see, the experience of separation actually creates an opening towards the state of enlightenment of Oneness realization. Don't be fooled by the ups and downs, the with or without, or the divided way; all frequency paths lead to the Oneness of All or the Unity of Consciousness.

There are many beautiful experiences in the separation state, for even there you carry the soul imprint of Unity Consciousness. It is often heart activation that begins to nudge you towards non-separation. Heart development is not only one of the most direct paths to Unity Consciousness due to its autonomous ability to swell and multiply its path, but the sublime power of the High-Heart is prepared and destined to be the main harbinger of all pursuits thereafter. Human incarnations provide great opportunities for Heart Expansion and within this potentiality lies the most potent path for Ascension from 3D to 5D. The heart provides the symphonic sounding pathway towards Cosmic Reunification but unfortunately, on this present Earth plane, the separation paradigm has become more devoid of the magnificence of the human heart. Instead, many humans see the outside world as stimulation for either something they need to have or something they need to protect against. "Needing to have" resonates from a place of diminishment and "needing to protect" resonates from a place of peril and fear. Remember, resonating frequencies determine how you vision the world around you. Ironically, understanding separation brings one closer to feeling the truth of the fifth dimensional plane, for in separation you have lived with fears, anxieties, aloneness, abandonment and helplessness.

So much time and space are utilized to secure external attachments and power to stave off the states of separation. Of course, when you only create half of the equation, either by external attachments, leaving out the "one" (you) or creating a world where you are the only one, shirking all others, Unity Consciousness cannot be experienced. The very attachment to another to stave off separation fears only creates more separation fears, as you secretly feel alone and in wait for further detaching, severing experiences. As humans live in separate material forms, daily living tasks surround creating security for that very material form. Survival of the "one" becomes paramount, leading the way for all else. *The current paradox of your planet is that the survival of the "one" is now totally dependent on the Unity of the All.* This becomes the natural procession of Consciousness evolution. Not all intelligent species lose the Unity memory when born into a material form, although there are incarnations where such loss is inherent in the species as a learning classroom to bring Unity to that which has been separate. Every time the "one" utilizes free will to join the flight of consciousness towards Unity, Source Intelligence expands the multidimensional Universe(s). You see, there is great purpose to your separation paradigm. You are born apart by the very experience of material form only to experience the shattering effects of total separation so that you might once again manifest the fires of free will to turn towards the face of Divinity. You have come to experience the self within so that you might utilize this beauteous self to synchronize and entrain with the beauteous Cosmos!

Remember, you cannot recognize or realize something outside of you that is not within you. You are experiencing the intense classrooms of Earth life so that you can indeed discover beauty, strength, peace, love and empowerment, thereby lighting up the resonating templates for magnifying those exact same experiences outside of yourself. Now, imagine an intimate encounter with "other than you" where safety, joy, curiosity and love become the only vibrational pathways for experiencing that "other." Vision a world where everything is beautifully safe, peaceful and abundant. In this revering state within your acute total awareness, know that you have never been separate from the All. You are resonating with the Unity of All, creating the movement towards the New Paradigm of the Ascending Earth. Your planet depends on this to survive. *What a paradox, to come to Earth and feel you must protect the "one" at all costs only to realize as you come to the expansive edges of evolution, you must protect the All in order for the "one" to survive!*

In the Unity experience of the Fifth Dimension, differences are celebrated and revered as proof of the great Source Architect. There is nothing outside of the Universal Oneness! Life is simply lived with this golden "knowing." It is the flight out of dualism, into wholeness. When you truly realize that both sides of the coin live in the same domain as you, you might begin to explore and take up residence in the whole of the coin. You have a saying, "The whole is more than the sum of the parts." Nothing is to be divided out; however, we realize that many humans feel that dividing things out is the process they use to try to make those very things disappear! Paradoxically, they appear more clearly when separated because you then see the very differences that inspired you to separate them in the first place. Unfortunately, the very differences solidify your false notion of separation. Usurping time and space to erect blockades creates dividing lines and partitions that becomes the very glue that holds the two sides together! It may be a little bit sobering to some to know that you are joined with the very things that divide you! To us, it is simply the immense diversity of Source Creation found in the Cosmic Strings of Oneness. In the 5D, there are no dividing lines, no dichotomies, no separate subdivisions. Safety and trust issues are simply unnecessary and, therefore, nonexistent.

EXPERIENCES IN THE FIFTH DIMENSIONAL REALM

1. You have infinite awareness that you always have been and will be connected with Source.
2. All beings have Source Spark within.
3. Conscious Resonation with your own Source Spark invites a Figure 8 with all other enlivened Source Sparks.
4. Diversities, whether in galactic form or individual designs, are celebrated and seen as crucial classrooms for holding in reverence the Grand Design.
5. Surviving of the "one" is measured by the surviving of the "All."
6. Cooperation takes on Cosmic meanings.
7. Nothing inhibits love, and sisterhood, brotherhood, cooperation, sharing, being, caring and evolving are hallmark signatures.
8. Self-awareness and selflessness become the material for the Figure 8 of Unity.
9. Joy and rejuvenation come from the Consciousness of the "one" resting in the arms of the All.
10. Invigoration and expansion of the "one" are discovered in the experience of the "other."
11. That which fuels you comes from the you in the All.
12. There are no fears of separation because you no longer are separate and, therefore, the reasons for such fears vanish.
13. Curiosity and inquisitiveness flow like a steady rapid stream of light. Ah, to be curious about that which is within you and that which surrounds you without fear or fret is truly sublime.

Seeing the world as an add-on, never a subtraction as in jealousy, anger, fear, is quite a shifting force. So everything you see has purpose, wonder, interest, wisdom. After all, those forces that cause such destruction on Earth are partly because they have not been seen with purpose, wonder, interest, wisdom and, most importantly, with love. You see without this "high vibe" resonation, those things indeed become more separate and more destructive. *It is not that destructive, dark forces simply disappear in the 5D, it is that the reason for them disappears.* Darkness is created because light has been withheld from it. It does seem to be true that when humans spend too much time in the dark shed, they can come up with some pretty disruptive, dangerous tools. When you begin to see the world through Unity Consciousness, you then bestow upon that world the frequency of that Lighted State. In this illuminated frequency, the darkness is diminished as it begins to vibrate with the ribbons of Unity Light. In making this transition, the most difficult part is to steadily embrace this irradiated truth while the world may indeed fall apart all around you.

In the Fifth Dimension, you have realized consciousness that you are vibrating in a sea of Universal Source Energy and are adrift in the fabric of it All. At that moment of Now Awareness, you gravitate towards that very place in others. Ah, to feel your own divineness and also to feel another's light at the same moment is true ecstasy! In the 5D, as you vibrate your highest frequencies within, you create a new template by which you can see the world and a close up, in-depth view of all that is sacred in All That Is. *The gravity or dynamic magnetism of the Cosmic Being moves and attracts from the inside out.* The frequencies within propel one to see resonant fields of surrounding energy. You can get closer to "God" by being closer to that One within, and you can get closer to the One within by seeing the All of Everything. Frequencies create your reality! See yourself as part of the Whole, and the Whole will be a part of you. Therefore it goes, that truly seeing the "holiness" in another is also part of seeing the "holiness" in yourself as all others hold the Whole of it All. As you merge the "one" of you to the One of All, you co-create an expanded, evolutionary lighted moment of the resounding (never heard before) lyrical notes in the Lighted Symphony of Source Consciousness. *Thus the One multiplies by its very creation of the "ones" as the "ones" travel on the slipstreams of free will to divine the creative powers within to move and awaken higher consciousness in the outer contours of the material world.*

It is important to note here that as you have this beautiful experience of "coming home" during this incarnated life, you will set the "stage" for the compete dissolving of Unity Consciousness amnesia in any life to come. Your current life, as well as many other incarnate lives, have prepared you for the big one…this time, this life, this Now. We know that although it has been a most grueling process to find your way back home, it is a great cosmic celebration, creating ripples throughout the Universe! You might say the energy or fuel that has been released from this life process ensures your safe passage into the multidimensional realms of Unity Purpose. You might want to pause here and appreciate just who you really are! ♡

Soul Sensory Modalities

It is most important to realize that I am utilizing your language in these pages to generate pathways to the trace memories of the many invisible realities you have already experienced. Although they have been relegated to the deep core of your higher consciousness, your cosmic gifts and "magical powers" are now ready to be released and remembered. Your human mind operates and resonates with written expression or "sounded" speech, spread in sacred design for your higher consciousness to follow, seeking explanation of the things that appear more ethereal and misty. Living in the 3D world, it seems that experiences of etheric qualities require a reality check or an interchange of resonation. Language provides this, moving and reinforcing the real "material" of spiritual Ascension. As the tool of verbal interchange is used to define and redefine, the hope is that you become more and more conscious of those out of time/space experiences that are already occurring within your home of higher consciousness. This in turn will produce more transforming pathways in language and description for others on your Earth plane to follow.

As you move into these new destinations, you will put language to work as I do, expanding the boundaries by which these things become everyday speech and experience. As these words make valid the recognition process of these experiences lying deep within, you will be able to produce the codes and essences necessary for your fellow human race. *So I say to you, as you continue to interact with the following pages, know there is nothing new to you, only openings to that which you have already experienced.* This is a most extraordinary and resplendent time on Earth! Close your eyes and just pause to feel this truth. ♡

As you open to this, you are in this moment unfurling the many seeded codes within. What an auspicious time. As the magnitude of cosmic light intensifies, it streams through the dissolving veils of your world. This light provides the fuel, the stimulus, the codes and the brightening agents for this Ascension time on your Earth. Who can argue with that which the Heavens bring! The good news is now it is upon you to utilize your own depth of knowing to allow these expanding, illuminated energies to "dial up" your light frequency quotient for the Ascended times to come. In this process, DNA is metamorphosed as dormant areas of your entire genome are being "lit up" and turned on to bring new, magical essences to your very being. You might say that learning to utilize these essences is the unwrapping of these gifts.

Many of these "waking" codes both within and surrounding you now, magnify and amplify what you have called extrasensory perception (ESP)...what we call *Soul Sensory Modalities (SSM)*. You have called ESP the ability to perceive things that are not readily available in your time and space paradigm. Of course, then it would make sense that moving from the Third to the Fifth Dimension would, by definition, require *extra sensory perception* as this is exactly what will enable you to "see and feel" the invisible world you are about to enter. You now have available through the downpouring of galactic illuminated frequencies, the "turning on" process for your *Soul Sensory Modalities.* You see, within your Soul Matrix you have astounding gifts, codes and essences gathered from many incarnations and parallel lives.

Regardless of the particular material configurations of various lives and experiences, you store within your Soul Matrix abilities to "sense," see, hear, touch, feel and intuit, and these soul-inherited endowments move across boundaries of time and space.

Each incarnation offers particular essences that enhance *Soul Sensory Modalities (SSM)* and require you to adapt to the material body of that particular domain. The denser the realities, the more difficult it is to have access to your higher, Source-endowed *SSM* abilities. Regardless of any one particular life lived, you have many beautiful, magnificent and magical "powers" stored within your Soul Matrix. You have seen humans throughout time who have had direct access to these amazing "soul gifts." Bilocation, levitation, telepathy, psychokinesis, remote viewing and clairvoyance are to name but a few. Although you have revered many humans who have demonstrated these gifts, it surprises us that you still don't realize you yourselves have access to them! If even one human on your planet demonstrates the manifestation of *SSM,* then this makes it possible for any human to actualize them. When one human accomplishes any of these higher manifestations, it signifies that the human genome is in fact capable of downloading and generating such extraordinary powers. Indeed, there are mighty potent essences that the 3D human genome simply cannot hold and actualize. You would not even be able to dream these things. However, know that if you can imagine and vision these *SSM* gifts, this is the first step in lighting the path for manifestation. Imagination and visioning all originate from higher consciousness; therefore, when some gifted code is ready to unfurl and become apparent, your Consciousness must first establish a template for this unfolding. Dreaming, visioning and imagining all provide the material for such arrangements to be embedded within your current incarnate being. In a way, you might say that dreaming, visioning and imagining are part of your original "human wiring" so that you might have the prerequisites necessary for awakening *Soul Sensory Modalities.* They open channels of communication between your higher self and your Soul Matrix, and through these channels flow the gifts.

Direct experience is the crème de la crème of "knowing" consciousness and the defining factor in the transformation of a species. Direct experience creates a state of being that opens the evolutionary highways within. If we came to teach you from the outside in, that spark within you might not be ignited unless you had total access to the entire direct experience by means of gathering with us. (For many, it would not be possible to "remember" such experiences because there is no belief in their existence.) As Source gave you complete sovereignty, this momentary unfurling must happen within you, by you and for you. For instance, seeing a galaxy through pictures is astoundingly different than experiencing a galaxy. For that matter, knowing the truth of extraterrestrial civilizations is quite different than meeting and experiencing a being from the cosmic neighborhood! When you see a picture of two people loving each other, the power of the picture will depend on whether you have had a direct experience of love. You see, the very manifestation of direct experience designs a beautiful, weaved fabric of vibrations forever available for resonating with that reality or frequency. Direct experience establishes all highways, pathways and portal openings to the *Connected Synchronistic Cosmic Web (CSCW). Direct Realization of these Soul Sensory Modalities is the grounding tool for importing new Ascended Energies to Earth!*

All phenomena of *Soul Sensory Modalities (SSM)* can be discovered on the slipstreams of the *Connective Synchronistic Cosmic Web (CSCW)* of the Universe. Telepathy, for instance, is simply connecting to the "etheric internet" of the "being mind network" flowing through the *CSCW.* Remote viewing is the ability to connect with the inner maps of the outer world manifestations in the *CSCW*. Psychokinesis is the ability to communicate with an object through frequency fields to produce a dance of movement. Mediumship is being able to ride the circuitry of the *CSCW* to what might be called the spirit realms. Precognition or clairvoyance is the ability to take a ride on the slipstreams and the potential destiny paths of your future world through time/space warps. Past life experiencers access frequency highways of the higher self to other living lives through the Soul Matrix. Many on your planet can communicate with our extraterrestrial family through a combination of these networks. The most crucial aspect of developing these most magnificent gifts is establishing the capability of seeing, feeling, sensing, tasting, touching and hearing phenomena that lives in the Fifth Dimension! Remember, everything is frequency and as you access this ability to refine your higher fields of *SSM*, channels to the beautiful, buoyant, multidimensional realms open. You brought many of these "gifts" with you when you incarnated into this Earth plane, and these were designed by you because you contracted and drafted the blueprint for this current Ascended Mission. You might think of these gifts as necessary tools in the transmutation process of becoming a 5D being!

All beings are conjoined in full consciousness to the *Connective Synchronistic Cosmic Web* in the Fifth Dimension and, therefore, *Soul Sensory Modalities* are simply alive and vibrantly spinning networks of reciprocity and resonation. As you begin to develop Source Given Gifts, a more common frequency language to understand extraterrestrial communication, celestial presence and Source Principles will also evolve. You are here because you have a widened field of cosmic sensory perception. You already have the cosmic antennas and aerial receivers downloading in rapid succession even more cosmic light codes of the Universe. *Developing the awareness that you already travel in these slipstreams is the key.*

It is important to point out that indigenous cultures, as well as cloistered spiritual communities, have produced an environment where humans have learned to effortlessly ride slipstreams to other realities. Shamans, for instance, have been the *CSCW* "seers" offering the human species a glimpse into other dimensional realities and magical realms. It is interesting to us that when an external device like the telescope or microscope is invented, the majority of humans become overnight believers in these previously noted invisible realms. Shamans, on the other hand, have known and traveled in the vast world of cosmic instrumentation that lies within the human domain, revealing many realities beyond galaxies and cells! As a human species, you have this power and will soon discover that you are capable of journeying within the vast network of *CSCW* to explore many new landscapes of consciousness! You might say that developing *SSM* is the organic diet of the Fifth Dimension.

BILOCATION: THE PATH IN

Bilocation of Consciousness is the most climacteric and pivotal *Soul Sensory Modality.* All other modalities thrive and flourish within the state of realized Conscious Bilocation. The reality is that you are already in many places and many times all at once, at least in your consciousness even if not yet in your awareness. Let's look at your current consciousness. At certain levels, the light quotient necessary for actual "material" bilocation has not yet been accomplished in the majority of humans. Your consciousness wakes in this one particular incarnation, so it feels you are always when and where you are in this particular time/space soul embodiment. The idea of being in two different physical localities seems rather impossible, even though you have many incidences of evolved humans doing so. The good news is that these cosmic gifts are within your grasp as the Earth and her inhabitants are moving through the Ascension Consciousness Revolution.

As human consciousness is being catapulted into the new reality of 5D cosmic physics, we might expect miraculous new abilities therein. It is important to know that bilocation of consciousness occurs quite frequently within your experiential domain and this is paramount to the process of material bilocation. Let's use the building blocks of your own quantum science to understand the mechanics of bilocation. Who and how reality is observed determines what reality you observe. Human consciousness then is the driver of the reality show and has enormous power to birth phenomenal substantiality. You might say that reality comes into form through the master observer of Consciousness. This is key in understanding the Ascension process before you. You have been ensconced in programs that say, "you are a **result** of the reality around you," diminishing both your power and free will. Consciousness is your cosmic passport towards the ultimate freedom of creation and manifestation. *As you begin to incorporate the myriad stratifications of your consciousness, you will know the experience of bringing reality into being and determining what that reality is.* But remember, you have been wedded to how your external life (science, religion, family, culture, etc.) has formed your ability to observe. Some people refuse to see the truth that lies in front of them (often called denial) and others see things no one else sees (often called delusions). Both are actually important experiences, as the first allows you to step out of corporeal realities and the other to step into invisible realities. The prime directive, however, is to sacredly and actively honor the *sovereignty* of your Consciousness. As you become the master of your domain of *realized awareness,* you unseal and release the powers and gifts that lie within the vital spark of evolutionary enlightenment. Bilocation is one of those cosmic-seeded gifts. For all things that have been invented, discovered and made anew on Earth have been channeled through those humans who have dared to walk in the mystery zones of unknown destinations with Awakened realization.

Consciousness gains momentum through the accelerated process of increasing the light quotient within. *What a beautiful reality-filled metaphor: increased illumination unfurls and amplifies the far reaches of the burgeoning Universe within and around you.* Of course, you have to experience the sublime state of the Here and Now before you can know you are everywhere. That is why the art of bilocation is so incredibly important at this time. As you become acutely aware that your consciousness is a capable traveler through practiced experience, you will be able to access, with fluidity and ease, the other *SSM.* As you travel on the Path of Ascension and increase the Source Radiance of your Soul Senses, you will be able to experience the lightness of being necessary for embracing two realities at once.

Bilocation of consciousness is a phenomenon you have already experienced. Traveling down the highways of your physical world, you might have noticed that you are able to "know" how and where you are going, yet find yourself daydreaming along the way, passing the exit gate for the final destination! Some of you are voracious daydreamers, allowing your consciousness to be somewhere else, all the while sitting in some meeting or classroom, half there and half not. Yet, daydreaming and imagination have often been discouraged in favor of unimagined, undreamt terrains of the programmed world. Who knew you were simply accessing a slipstream for bilocation and, therefore, illuminated consciousness! The ability to dream, imagine and vision amplifies and expands your frequency library, creating more resonant fields of recognition and knowledge. As you experience your imagination, know that new channels for cosmic wisdom and the multidimensional worlds are being opened. Spend time allowing your consciousness to go beyond this time/space dimension. Do not confuse *being here now*, as an obstacle to imagination, vision and dreaming. *The Now simply provides the frequency quotient necessary for generating the buoyancy required for consciousness travel to All That Is.* Remember, *being here now* in pure consciousness produces the alchemy for manifesting all *Soul Sensory Modalities (SSM)*.

Most of you engage in consciousness bilocation through dream channels and "dreamtime" during sleep is more than it seems. As you experience dreaming, it is not just a brain phenomenon to wash away the dross of the day; in many instances, higher consciousness is utilized to travel outside of your body. Some call this astral travel. An exact energetic duplicate of your physical body is able to travel beyond the material body, all the while still residing within the whole of your Soul Matrix. Much of what is encountered in the astral realm is connected with your current dimension of experience and so you often roam the current time/space continuum of the Earth realm.

Another nighttime activity involving bilocation of consciousness is the art of lucid dreaming. This is an incredible example of the "realized awareness" of bilocation, where you become fully aware that you are dreaming while in a sleep state. As a result, the totality of the dream landscape can be changed, creating textures and outcomes previously unavailable in the non-lucid state. Learning to lucid dream is a wonderful way of consciously placing yourself in the dream so that you might decide and create exactly what happens. This is a most important endowment to practice because it increases the ability to be consciously aware of the "both of you" while bilocating consciousness. Bringing your awareness to dreamtime is a beautiful way to know that you are both awake and asleep, and yet the overriding arc of consciousness can be in both places at once.

Bilocating the body is just the next step of several. Shifting into two locations requires lifting a duplicate copy of the entire you to a different place and slightly different time. Your consciousness has to be more and more infused with the soulic light matrix so that light consciousness is capable of lifting the physical body in duplicate form to another location. "Light consciousness" is the only power that can overcome the gravitational pull of the material realities while holding steady the realization of the many realities. This is a high-level soul modality. Humans that accomplish this are more Soul Light than body and so can move material form. It is interesting that some of you have done this without consciously remembering. Remembering is a brain activity in humans and, therefore, when transported out of time/space the brain often is simply not recording this, as it does not have the circuitry or data entry points for such experiences. Your human mind may not register these experiences because the physical brain is wired to hold time/space signposts of waking experiences. This 3D "data" is qualitatively different from the vibrational experiences of higher consciousness that take place in dreamtime or eventually in "waking higher consciousness events." The *Soul Sensory Modalities*, like bilocation, operate in the fifth dimensional realm and, therefore, are "frequency/energetic experiences" rather than particular coded data bites. The regular human brain has yet to develop "holding stations" for these "frequency experiences" to be stored, let alone remembered.

One of the most exciting and enchanting events taking place in the human species is the ability to expand Consciousness Circuitry. This new circuitry is being enveloped and fueled by the Cosmic Light that is currently streaming into the Earth plane. As consciousness awakening is sparked and stirred, the star-seeded DNA within the fabric of your living material is aroused and stimulated. This, in turn, enhances and cultivates the "new circuitry" that inspires and enables your ability to embrace and hold in place your consciousness during the effervescent travels of bilocation. You will not only be able to reserve these Soul Sensory journeys in the new circuitry, but will also be able to learn how to move in the new consciousness networks, gaining access to all the altered states of conscious experience you have ever had. Oh, what a time is coming! Therefore keep in mind, you are experiencing many more of these "altered" states of consciousness than you know. At the precise moment that it is taking place you may have total awareness of this experience but, without the new holding circuitry, recall will be difficult. Until the neo-circuitry of the 5D mind is thoroughly established, these split consciousness experiences can create fugue states, where you may experience difficulty coming back into this time and place. Even daydreaming or imagination practices are bilocation experiences that can cause you to feel like you are returning from some foreign expedition where it is then difficult to register current time/space differentiation. Once back, you may experience hypomnesia, or the forgetting of these "break out" experiences.

There is a zone or field in between these "split" realities that keeps you connected and apart all at once…let's simply call this the "energetic band in between realities." This zone is a bridge that provides access as well as differentiation of the distinct voluminous reality experiences. As you traverse towards these new fifth dimensional realities, you journey through this threshold of connective, vibrational, soul material where both worlds can appear a bit hazy and disorienting. Upon passing through this band, whatever world you travel to becomes clear and apparent. Realized awareness of both realities all at once is the key to bilocation travel. Lighted Consciousness within the Soul Matrix creates many material lifetimes, so it follows that as you evolve to higher, overarching, consciousness realities you have access to these new soul destinations. Continue to imagine, vision, daydream, lucid dream, astral travel and, most of all, live in the High-Heart Consciousness so that you may simply be more fully in the frequencies of Ascension.

Imagine or vision consciousness as a light vibrational grid. As you tune in and turn on your illuminated ribbons of *realized awareness* the grid becomes beautifully enlivened with undulating fractals of light. And, as this field becomes brilliantly expanded, the buoyancy provides access points to the matrix where multidimensional phenomena can be experienced. There are various techniques on your planet that already point the way to this bilocation process. For instance, Quantum Healing Hypnotic Regression prescribes a method for accessing past lives of different incarnations. As an altered state of consciousness is created through trance states, the slipstreams that carry you to other lives at other times and places are able to be entered. This can have enormous healing benefits, but even more profound is consciously "crossing over" to the infinite Universe and the multidimensional layers of the One (the All of You). It is the same with experiencing "bleed throughs" from parallel life exploration. In this process, recognition of different destiny potentialities that exist can emerge, albeit in other worlds or Universes. In these kinds of experiences, conscious bilocation via the quantum reality of the Soul Matrix is happening already. When you begin to explore past lives and parallel realities, the frequency pathways for actual bilocation of this incarnate self on Earth will be initiated. *Remember, this beautiful most astounding Soul Matrix holds the All of You, all incarnations, all parallel lives and cosmic codes and essences; therefore, this is where your higher consciousness is merged and connected to the potentialities living in all dimensions, as well as to the Greater Universal Soul Source.*

Know that your parallel and incarnate lives not only exist but also are a tremendous element of affecting and influencing your life now. A more lively discussion on this will follow in the next chapter, but suffice it to say that you have distinct, concurrent incarnations as well as same life parallel realities. These parallel and incarnate lives are simply in a different Universe and for now you may only see the one you are in. It is all happening simultaneously, but typically without your conscious awareness. Bilocation is a frequency journey where the light of consciousness is able to travel across Universes with cognizance of different states of being. Lighted consciousness is able to bypass the material world, seeing and observing the amazing verity of many lives in different time/space frames and alternate destiny paths. This lighted consciousness lives in your Soul Matrix and you might say that Soul Matrix creates the strands of lighted material for the living experiences necessary towards Soul Enlightened Source Awareness. Each life created is an expansion of the frontiers of Source Intelligence, all the while spiraling back to the totality of Divine Source. As your own consciousness evolves, its light quotient increases and becomes more capable of traveling on the slipstreams of this illuminated matrix. So, you might begin to see that bilocation is simply the ability to consciously observe and witness more of the "one" (all that you are) and more of the One (All That Is). Mind-blowing and awe-inspiring all at once...for as you move closer to the "one" of many, you begin to become more wholly aware and of the One.

PHYSICAL SENSES TURN SOULFUL

THE SOUND OF THE LIGHTED PATH

Sounds embrace a healing frequency for the material world in which they live. Can you hear beyond your physical ears and feel the wisdom that speaks at a higher vibrational level? The wind whispers a sweet message of the higher matrix of nature. Listen to a stream and you will begin to hear a symphony of sounds...different notes created by each passing rock and the full chorus of water running rich and deep. Embedded in your nature are phenomenal sound-designs for your Ascension journey. Nothing is an accident as the Divine channels of higher energy become materialized in nonrandom fashion. Listen to the natural abundance of Earth's megacosm and hear the song of the wind, the ballad of the birds, the wisdom of the trees and the rhythm of the rain. There are sacred patterns in every sound. Use your hearing to bring them in and utilize your heart to know their wisdom. Nature is such an important practice field for "soul hearing," which is the ability to hear sounds through feeling the heart and echoing the sounds. Rejuvenation through these higher-sounding templates is quite remarkable. A brief journey into nature's bounty will produce this enchanting, alchemic experience, as this sounding quest magically smooths and expands the edges of previously confined harmonic spaces. The full hearkening resonance of tonality and sonority can then be discovered and celebrated.

Within the sound of living things, there can be found the veracity of their very core of Beingness. You see, everything has a sound blueprint, including you! Through the sound of the human voice, the hidden deeper truths can be felt within and laying in wait to be gently held and heard. Can you hear the sounded blissful notes of your love for one another? You may access the many "sound libraries" of music, colors, numbers…even beings. Listen to Earth's music creators and pause to feel the corridor openings to other realities. Your planet has a unique, beautiful tone of cosmic sound; let yourself explore that vibration in your belly. Hear the sounding Universe through the vibrational rippling within your body and heart. See movement and hear the sound of it simply by the dancing flow. Begin to hear the whispers of guides and teachers who live in other dimensional realms. Higher ET and Celestial Beings surrounding your planet often utilize sound as a method of communication. Tones, ringing in the ear, strange anomalous whispers and euphonious rhythms can all be heard. Listen carefully and you may hearken an angelic chorus in the wings of your awareness. These sounds stimulate your awakening DNA codes and enliven your star-seeded genome to reverberate with your resounding higher consciousness, thus propelling you into the Fifth Dimension.

Simply pause to listen to the silence of quiet stillness and plan to be surprised. You will begin to heed the hushed tones of sacred designs and the cosmic harmonics therein.

SEEING THE LIGHTED PATH

Let us start with the *belief* that there is indeed more to *see* than the eyes can perceive. This belief becomes the keyhole by which you can peek and behold the rich template of all there is to see! Know that as you begin to see through your visual *Soul Sensory Modality*, beliefs will become magnified and multiplied exponentially thereby creating more sighted vision. Developing your "sight" into the invisible realm is a most exquisite and expansive process. As you begin to "see" the truth beyond your current paradigm, you will lead the way for accelerated movement into the beyond thus making known that which was previously unexplored. These previously uncharted territories and vistas then become less yielding to the old habitual thinking or visual patterns of standard archetypes of past times. Once new realities are seen and therefore felt, it is most impossible to pretend to be amaurotic or unsighted. This is the good news!

Light sources can be measured as many different wavelengths of energy on the light spectrum. Humans see a very small range of this whole visual light spectrum (there are more light frequencies yet to be measured on your scientific spectrum). In fact, the human visible light spectrum is infinitesimal compared to oscillating light spectrums in the Cosmos. And yet, with this spectacular evolutionary time on Earth, the human vision is experiencing its own revolution. Accessing the ability to "see" into what you might call the invisible spectrum is indeed possible. Auras, lighted orbs and fluxing energy fields are examples of the human capability in peering beyond the spectrum. The third eye, what we call the "passkey" for magical vision, and the human physical eye are experiencing a form of merging. The third eye, once activated, can see past the veil of illusion of your material world and into the ethereal world where the energetic body holds the higher consciousness realms of Soul Matrix. The ability to see and "know" these higher dimensional realms can most certainly be found in the third eye experience. Imagination is a most potent and integral aspect for accessing and stimulating the portal of the third eye. After all, *imagination produces the corridor by which all other dimensions can be found.*

The third eye chakra is being rapidly activated in your human species, as the cosmic grid of light is most potently enveloping your planet. These incoming, coded, light frequencies stimulate and dilate the energy/etheric meridians surrounding and within your material body. Thus, the third eye chakra is plump with illuminated potentialities. *As you begin to vision that which is beyond your material world, impressions are established that become available to the patterning of stenciled pathways overlaid onto your material visual capabilities.* The physical eye thereby has new, expanded abilities to see beyond that which has been seen in the material plane. As the magical third eye opens and creates these conduit paths of lighted information, it provides yet a larger pathway for the lighted codes to stimulate your genome. This newly activated cosmic DNA initiates a coalescing process with the body and your higher consciousness to produce a commingling of the spirited light world with your physical world. And this "new you" is part of the Ascension journey. Lo and behold, you "see" a whole new world! You then have the capacity to visualize the new 5D world through this mystical process of blended spirit/material sight realities. The moment the light merges with the material, it signals your cosmic DNA codes to turn on and tune in, making room for the light/material circuitry to come. It is surrounding you now…can you begin to cultivate the sight to see? ♡

What might you begin to see? This transformation will not only effect what you visibly see, but will open channels to behold the wisdom held within the visual information itself. In other words, *you will be able to see something and intuit in the seeing the information within the seeing.* The very act or experience of the new vision immediately catapults and transforms the one who is seeing! For instance, as you initiate a conscious relationship with the trees of your planet by pausing and becoming an *awake-witness* to them, you begin to intuit their telepathic communication. As you sense this connection, you may eventually develop the ability to see and feel their vibrational fields emanating towards you. Perhaps you will perceive a sudden, perceptible breeze on your face or, more importantly, you might take notice of the quivering, rooted pulse in the heart of your being. After all, if you don't create the interlude of pause from which you can look, the gates of acknowledgement, communication and inner reception will never open. Seeing with your soul sense may turn on other etheric senses as well, as you may taste the aroma of the tree's leaves and energetically touch the essence of its contoured body.

As the physical eye becomes merged with the magical third eye, your sight will have great capacity to travel into the slipstreams of higher consciousness and the *Connective Synchronistic Cosmic Web (CSCW)*. You will begin to see the world in more vibrant, intense colors, including auras, sacred designs and energetic lighted contours surrounding living things. In addition, you will develop the sight to "see" the presence of other living beings, as your surrounding space may be illumined with orbs of light, fluxing and undulating trails of lighted energy and even illuminated energy bodies. You will be able to vision the higher frequency realms of the Fifth Dimension as a result of adapting to this new "seeing." ET craft and lighted displays will be noticeable in the skies above you; however, those who haven't opened these lighted abilities will simply not see these. This will present quite a quandary for many of you! You see, moving into fifth dimensional consciousness is developing *evolutionary vision*. In this quest, you will see a most expanded and quite magical world that will begin to feel more real and amazing than the world of 3D restricted sight and sound. Remember, this revolutionary process requires the Now resonance of Consciousness in order to ground here (in this incarnate form) and travel there (multidimensional realms) all at once. This most certainly is an example of the *bilocation of conscious vision*. Remaining in the

material world of incarnate presence while visioning beyond time/
space boundaries is such an amazing and crucial part of Ascension.
If you are residing anywhere else than the crystal clear moment of
NOW, you are simply in the phenomenon of time/space variables
where regular 3D vision presides and 5D vision fades. Come "see"
what extraordinary and magical worlds live in the Now presence of
All That Is! ♡

TELEPATHY: CONNECTING TO THE LIGHTED PATH

Telepathic communication is the one cosmic sensory modality
that is instrumental in attesting to the evolvement of a civilization.
Prior to arriving at the portals for such "invisible" connections, there
must be integrity of the highest spiritual intention and transparency of
one's deepest truth. In the human arena, there are so many competing
feelings and thoughts that arouse complicated and seemingly
incongruous and disjointed behaviors. These make it almost impossible
to begin to decipher the intuitive knowings about another's true inner
state. Time after time you may have the experience where you feel
someone's state of mind or heart, only to have them deny that it is so.
And, because humans are often in denial of their deepest motivations,
desires, emotions and wishes, it is easy to misstep amidst the somewhat
chaotic world within.

An amazing thing happens when you desire to open telepathic
channels. However, in order to be within the frequency essence that
creates the telepathic journey to the outer/inner boundaries of another,
you must first practice this journey within yourself. So it goes, those
initial practice sessions will entail uncovering and liberating yourself
from your own detritus and obscuring fields so that the deepest truth
of who and what you are might be intuited. If you are bewildered by
your own inner world, it no doubt confounds the process of telepathy.
As you vibrate in this deeper place within, you tap into the purest
essence of you, thus creating a resonant bridge to the purest essence
of the surrounding Universe. The saying, "know thyself to know all

else" is paramount in manifesting the beautiful experience of the Figure 8 of telethesia! As you begin to feel the deeper essences of you and, therefore, your Magnificence (because after all, the deeper, more remote places within you house the untouched cosmic version of you…without the debris of the 3D programs), you create a vibrational ripple that begins to resonate with all that is sacred about you.

You might first try communing with Earth's Nature, as that which is alive in the natural world has always maintained pure jubilance of Divine Presence. You will have such a delightful "trip" with these indigenous, innate elements of your planet, resonating with ease and delight in these "invisible" relations of kindred spirits. That which lives in your natural world has never lost its telepathic presence. How beautiful that your trees know your deepest truth. Walk within the trees and feel the total acceptance and strong presence they have with your Soul/Cosmic Self. Even though they hold within their collective consciousness field the harm humans have inflicted upon their sovereign province, the trees stand with grace before you and invite you to feel their majestic presence. And in turn, they feel the magnificence of your soul's predilections, stirring that place within that you have long kept hostage. This most beautiful, organic process present in studying the deepest, magnificent realms of the self organically births a pathway spinning outward towards your natural surroundings for practicing and developing the new habitudes for telepathic travel.

There may be a time when Earth's electronic communication networks are not available and then it will be most crucial that you have innate telepathic networks up and running. Transparency and honesty are the most crucial elements in accelerating the human telepathic learning curve. As you clear your field and surround yourself with those who are on the same revelational path, you will be amazed how quickly this skill can be developed. After all, it is inherent in the very fabric of your being. Let it move within you and feel the presence of the Cosmic Web within and surrounding you. Each individual houses this cosmogonic switchboard. Did you not know you were a *cosmic operator?*

Can you begin to recognize our communication with you? Have no doubt...we are in constant contact telepathically. It is most amazing to be alert to the incoming calls that come from the starlit waves from the interlacing Universe. As you travel these inner and outer roads, note any physical sensations, emotional experiences and intuitive flashes when you approach some deep truth and soul knowing. Those are the "trace-keys" of the *telethesic frequency states* that you can recognize when you are receiving communication from others in your world or the Cosmos beyond. There are so many "trace-keys" surrounding you. In your dreams, you may come upon a landscape or gathering associated with a person in your past. You may not even identify with seeing them in the dream state but, as they are "thinking" of you, they are sending some deep feeling or connection that you "pick up" as a remnant of a place you traveled together. This as a telethesia frequency experience because that particular person does not come into your "awake" consciousness; however, the trace-key elements are there.

You would be quite surprised if you knew how much your higher consciousness registers pure, deep connections. It is just that the 3D human self also stores heavier, denser feelings, thoughts and memories of events and persons. There is a collision inside and direct telepathic communication becomes more arbitrary and, therefore, delayed and disrupted. As you become less judgmental and critical, and more whole within as a result, you will be able to dance with more grace among your human journeyers. The sacred enhancement of wholeness and "holiness" will provide an anointing salve to the broken, telepathic channels, creating clearer consciousness for the recognition of telethesia frequency states within and around you. In this recognition, you will begin to feel the Sacred Figure 8 of the connections between yourself and all that encompasses you. This, of course, is a most essential path to Unity Consciousness.

SYNCHRONISTIC ATTUNEMENT: LIVING IN THE LIGHTED PATH

As the *Soul Sensory Modality (SSM)* of telepathy increases, it provides a portal opening for the *SSM* we call Synchronistic Attunement. Many of you have been having experiences that might, at first, seem serendipitous. These accidental discoveries are actually the result of the Synchronistic Web appearing or breaking through the veils into your 3D world. The ability to feel and see these "break-through moments" signals that your Synchronistic Attunement sensory modality is up and running. Having developed a way of "tuning in" to the invisible realm, your own transforming, coded soul essences become more evident. As you experience this, a resonant energetic field that ripples out into this overarching, harmonic, universal network is created and this, in turn, establishes more congruous channels, echoing your readiness for this Attunement. Like a magnet, these openings allow more and more beacons of illuminated information to stream forth, signaling alignment with not only your higher self but indeed the universal network of higher energies.

People and situations that have important meaning, providing guidance and direction, have crossed your path. Symbols, numbers and sacred designs have come to your attention, stimulating your consciousness to see beyond or rather see "into" the vast Synchronistic Cosmic Web. There is so much that constantly bursts into your world from other realms, other beings and other frequency domains. Becoming an authentic decipherer of these higher communications is the key. Hold the Mantra: *Nothing is as it seems, but everything is a clue.* The vast cosmic network within becomes more apparent as your consciousness expands into this fantastical world of pointers, signs and keys. Now you are able to initiate the co-creative state of expanding the always-present, never-ending Universe. The human race is currently in the midst of many beautiful discoveries pertaining to this overarching synchronistic network. Revelations of the Fibonacci sequence, the golden ratio, string theory, quantum entanglement and the sacred geometric designs enveloped in the universal language of creation have been experienced. You are now understanding the intertwining of music, mathematics and planetary movement. You have discovered instrumentation providing the ability to see the most grand (space of galaxies) and the most infinitesimal worlds (quantum realities) and the relationship of the two. *These discoveries have been revealed to those humans who follow the almost imperceptible clues into the invisible world and see patterns where there was chaos, meaning where there was insignificance and revelation where there was obscurity.* All of this is testimony to the organizational principles within the *Connective Synchronistic Cosmic Web (CSCW).* Now you can enter the most amazing world where everything is within you and You become the device for inter and intra "seeing" and knowing.

Humans have the capability to see and experience the truths of this *CSCW* far quicker, developing external devices for such. There is something in the very aliveness of a being (human or other), something in their moving, spiraling light quotient that opens corridors to the vastness of the Universe. However, you must first feel the truth of that which requires you to know and feel your Magnificence, for this beautiful light is your Magnificence! It is this very Life Force that is the creator of all internal "devices" for seeing, feeling and knowing. *As you come to simply **be** this, you will open the corridors and enter the most extraordinary Network of Light, where limitless information spirals in circular motion, abounding with joyful revelations about the Universe around you and within you.* See that which surrounds you as an amazing design of Creative Divine Source and learn to follow the subtle trails of the synchronistic matrix of all living light. As you take nothing for granted and embrace all possibilities, you will open *Soul Sensory Modalities* with more ease and fruitful exploration. Follow the wisps of intuitive knowing, synchronistic happenings, telepathic experiences, dreaming while awake and the imaginative flashes of other realities. These are the slipstreams to the most extraordinary *Connective Synchronistic Cosmic Web!*

HEART DIVINATION: BEING THE LIGHTED PATH

The Sacred Heart has the ability to bring in curative Divine spirals, lighting the beauteous Ascension passageway. The wisdom that opens in the heart when the transformative *galactic diamond awakening* occurs is quite magnificent. You can feel it now…every time you see love in action, kindness surrounding you, connection where there has been none, unity where there was division and justice and equality where Earth's inhabitants are cherished and revered. *These are the High-Heart Activations opening the wisdom channels to all that is beyond, making possible the birthing of the New Earth.* Carry your heart everywhere you go; develop realized awareness of your High-Heart destiny and the soul yearning to live anew! Quickly disperse of the lower denser vibrations that your world sparks in the burning fires of your heated heart and rest assured that as you embrace your Higher Heart, you open the Sacred Channels of Heart Divination found at the very center of your soul. Feel the most magnificent sense of freedom and soaring as your heart creates the rhythms of Divine Crystalline Light of Unity and Love on Earth. You are the Bringer of the Dawn of the Celestial Heart and this is the quintessential Earth journey.

Allow the tenderness of such celestial touches of the High-Heart to soften the edges of your burdened self, freeing you from the 3D prisons of judgment, disbelief, sorrow, anger and hopelessness. These are simply illusions, my friends, to spark the re-awakening of your Divine Heart. You hold the magical alchemic cure for such illusionary chimeras fabricated in the material world of time/space, as you are the spark of the Divine Heart in human form. What a beautiful way for Source to continue to create through you, by Divining the Universes to come. You may say, "How do I evolve my heart when it is aching and tired?" We say, "Find someone to love today." Seek out an Earth inhabitant waiting for the healing of kindness and compassion. Bring a united spirit to those who have been pushed to the outer banks of disenfranchised imprisonment. Kiss a tree leaf or feel the wind on your cheek, and be blessed by the Earth's embrace. Reach out your hand to those who have forgotten they are worthy of touch. You have done these things many times before here and elsewhere…remember?

It is important to know that humans have a special "built in" connection with the merging channels of the material heart and the Soul Heart. Your species can be extraordinarily beautiful when Heart-led. There are ET Beings and Celestials surrounding Earth right now…just to witness this Awakening Heart of the Human Being. Many galactic species have lost this ability and so are here to learn from you. They are surprised that even though they see darkness on Earth when the human heart is shadowed, it still is able to rise and light the world. This *Soul Sensory Modality* is the one most natural to your Being of Humanness. Dissolve the protective covers, lead with your Heart and feel the strength of direction, conviction and inspiration.

Free will is a most-interesting phenomenon. A species can choose to hinder or excel with their exquisite gifts and assets. You might be surprised to learn that there are other planets in your cosmic neighborhood where *human species* live and prosper in Unity Consciousness. In many of those civilizations, they have chosen to acculturate and assimilate societies with High-Heart ministrations, creating designs that might look to you like a garden paradise not unlike Shangri-la. And, Shangri-la is a "real" place where fifth dimensional humans live in an invisible realm on Earth in total harmony, love and unity. This template is ever so crucial, as it creates an energetic field of potentialities much needed today on your planet. Oh, how beautiful these cosmic communities are! To see the High-Heart template of the human species in action is quite an amazing sight. It would both make you cry and leap with joy all at once. You may ask, "What happened on this planet to cause the human race to veer off track of the High-Heart?" Remember…free will.

Where there is choice, there is exploration, information and knowledge, all-important in the Enlightenment journey. It is paramount and essential that all realities of the light/dark heart spectrum be explored. You might say, the Earth paradigm of human realities has been somewhat stranded on the dark shadowy side. Suffice it to say, it is an amazing task to utilize your Lighted Consciousness to "chose" to find the light where there has been dark. It takes a great Light Warrior to realize that sacred volition lies within the sovereignty of the Heart, as it has the power to transform consciousness at a global and cosmic level. It may be hard to believe that darkness and denseness contain great lessons but they are the Ascension fuel for the journey towards your evolution.

The Earth is on the precipice of a Great Dawn. Humans have the most amazing opportunity to create the Illuminated Love Spiral... birthing new realities of Global Unity Consciousness into being. What an auspicious task. Do not be fooled by what you see outside of you, for this is a *personal-soul revolution*. Make your own choices, bring your own realized awareness of the truth of your amazing, illuminated Heart to bear on life on your planet. Do not look outward, but **be** the light that you are. Know that you are indeed enough...each choice, each movement of High-Heart action is most extraordinary. Many are watching, because it is unbelievable to see the Illuminated Heart being birthed from the ashes of repression, diminution and amnesia. Every time you act with High-Heart you send a ripple into the Universe that is fuel for Source Light beyond your imagination. This is the most crucial *SSM* for humans to develop in order for Earth to follow her own rhythmic Heartbeat of Ascended Power. For you will learn this most sacred of *Soul Sensory Modalities* and this shall lead the Earth. Open your Heart and let yourself fly above the noise, the din and the clamor. The High-Heart is filled with illuminated buoyancy to move beyond the gravitational pull of current human protocols of separation and division. As you act with love, kindness, unity, peace and compassion, you increase the potentialities of fifth dimensional realities to burst forth, showering All with Abundance and Joy. Remember, it will not be hard to be in this "hearted residence" as you have already experienced that many times; it will only be hard to walk with this in these times before you and embrace all who are lost. Perhaps the lost have been there to stir these truths within you so that you may return and remember your High-Heart mission…rousing and reveling the New Dawn of epic proportions on Earth.

FREQUENCY PROPAGATION: MULTIPLYING THE LIGHTED PATH

Becoming the consummate transcendent *frequency propagator* is the ultimate Ascended Mission on Earth. *A frequency propagator is simply someone who has the realized consciousness to be and proliferate their highest, most sacred frequency signatures, thereby creating a world where the illuminated path is apparent and invites those looking for the lighted way.* As these resonant frequencies become more abundant throughout the world, the vibrations of fifth dimensional Ascension will turn on and turn up. All humans emanate vibrational fields; however, most are oblivious to the breadth and depth of this motion of movement within and surrounding them. Thoughts, feelings and physical fields all produce oscillating and fluctuating wavelengths of invisible dynamism. Your science is beginning to study and is even developing devices to measure these frequency states. Understanding the veracity and power of these vibrating states of *being alive* is a crucial step in all civilized cosmic societies. The frequencies you create and radiate affect all that surrounds you and become the preeminent and most potent alchemic materials for either transformation or stagnation. Developing *realized awareness* of your frequency states, especially those emanating from the Heart center, is paramount at this time of Earth transformation.

Many humans ask me, "Could you help me know my mission?" I say, "This is your mission…to become a generator of your highest soul's sacred movement and simply walk in the world!" I tell you, "When you see your most evolved humans walking in the world, are they smiling? What does it feel like to walk past them or sit in their presence? Have you noticed that in the first moments of meeting someone who radiates this beauty, you feel such a magnetic attraction to them?" You have a resonation station within that holds and monitors the incoming frequency fields, guiding you with intuitive knowing towards movement or stillness. It may be happening without awareness, but it is operating in constant vigilance. No doubt there are such competing and, at times, chaotic external pulsations moving into your inner world, clogging the channels of clear awareness. This certainly makes it difficult to discern and fine-tune this process. Often, the amount of incoming information is so intense, constant and mountainous that numbness sets in making it difficult to regain your inner power. Know the current task is not to develop more discernment about the *outside-in flow* but rather to be more magnificent in the *inside-out flow*. Transparency, sacredness, truth, integrity of intent and consistency of flow are all important vehicles for this *inside-out flow*. The vibratory fields of the High-Heart will be the content within these undulating carriers that will transform and change the Earth!

There are four Mantras of Earth Mission:
1. I am a *frequency propagator*.
2. I will be aware and conscious of the frequency states that I generate.
3. I will be an active creator of the vibrational states within that I want to see in the world.
4. I will become a *World Walker* emanating these 5D frequencies to create the New Earth.

Mission, then, is to allow Consciousness to surround and reside in the soul-sacred resonant fields within and radiate these reverberations to all, thus creating *As Above, So Below*. No matter what you do, where you go, or whom you choose to be with, your mission is always present and potent. How beautiful, magnificent and uncomplicated all at once. As you become a *conscious frequency propagator*, the deeper cosmic essences and codes that you have brought to Earth will be turned on… just for this mission. This will make manifest the details of the lifeworks of your current incarnation. There will be more ease and centering on what you do and how it is done. You have so much incredible support, not only from higher ancestral and Celestial guides but from the very sacred material you brought with you to this amazing Ascension journey for this time and for this place.

THE MOST MAGICAL MOMENT OF NOW

It must be noted that without the entrance into the super-charged energies of the Now, creative power and frequency generation will be stifled and mired. The Now is the only "place" that holds the purity of stillness necessary for movement into the Fifth Dimension. The past and future are shrouded with details of data-filled *time-winks* that have lost their vibrancy and power. When Consciousness is fully experienced in the Here-Now, you enter the gates of the most powerful fuel available for the Ascension journey. This permits you to go past the current horizontal-incarnated form into the vertical-expanded world of All That Is. The Now has a very particular cosmic template frequency. As you manifest this vibrational field, portals open…streaming cosmogonic wisdom and connecting you with the *vast network of the infinite moments of Now.*

Being Here-Now is not just what you might call a psychological construct for rest and relaxation so that you might have a break from the thunderous onslaught of data-points that are flat and diminished. *It is a field of quantum awareness that allows you to be on the superhighway of All Else.* Now is a vibrational state that sends resonant signatures to the very core of the Universal Life Pulse, thus opening avenues to all that is beyond. If you are not in the Now, you are probably caught in the mires of 3D living, feeling the past or thinking the future. Find that stillness point in your mind and the open range of your Heart expanse. Only then will you feel the oscillations of the powerful, magical Now moment beckoning you with the infinite possibilities of being everywhere all at once. This is the elevator ride to the slipstreams of the Cosmic Web, surpassing the boundaries of your current incarnation and expanding your consciousness. Thus, you return to your *soul-home* where the All of You resides. ♡

As you begin to have expanded consciousness experiences, allow the mysterious unknown to become a familiar sensation, an acknowledged frequency or an intuitive wisp of wisdom. For these live in the beauteous template of the infinite Now, which is the fabric of quantum cosmic frequencies that can be found everywhere in your Universe. Feel the illuminating light in the Now matrix and encounter all that is within and beyond you. You will discover you are made of the same cosmic material found in every living thing. This is the truth of who you are!

All *Soul Sensory Modalities* that have been previously enshrouded by old paradigm programs and debris fields of human living can be found in the shimmering moment of Now. As *Soul Sensory Modalities* open in your human maturation of spirit, the soul journey becomes the tour de force and dynamic impetus for evolution and Ascension. These discoveries have been revealed to those humans who follow the almost imperceptible clues into the invisible world and see patterns where there was chaos, meaning where there was insignificance and revelation where there was obscurity. Many more will be opening for you as you walk this Ascension path. Here are just a few:

- ✦ Levitation is the lightening of the material body combined with the alchemic illumination of spirit.
- ✦ Remote viewing is exploring and perceiving the visible utilizing the invisible charted sight within.
- ✦ Clairvoyance is being in the frequency of high intuition where there is access to invisible time/space knowledge.
- ✦ Precognition is an ability to gain access to the slipstreams of future probabilities.
- ✦ Synesthesia is a sensory phenomenon where one perceptual pathway of experience triggers and stimulates other physical senses. For example, numbers elicit colors and months of

the year stimulate precise space locations. The human brain is capable of creating these neuron-sensory pathways as practice for 5D *Soul Sensory Modalities.* Synesthetes have gained access to this beautiful part of the human brain and are able to see into fifth dimensional realities as a result.

Allow your consciousness to ride the pathways of expanded awareness in the Now frequency grid and begin to see how the extrasensory modalities arise from the Soul Sensory template to create a spectacular array of New Paradigm realities. *Allow the smallest almost imperceptible awareness of the potentialities of your Soul Senses; if the little things do not change your life, you are probably not ready for the big things!* Follow the trail of mysterious feelings, sensations and intuitions and you will begin to explore new frontiers of the multidimensional Universe. Remember, this repositioning of the time/space continuum cannot happen without rearranging your **time** and your **space**. Time/space awareness has particularly been arranged to incorporate the 3D parameters, which often omit the Now experience. Pause to see the anchors and cues in life that direct your Awareness to the "out of Now" experience. Rearrange your life to incorporate more stillness, expanding your effervescent consciousness field into the elusive corners of the *Now-corridors*…flowing into the experience of the Oneness of Being!

A Descriptive Journey into the Fifth Dimension

Body, mind, heart and spirit are in sacred-alignment in wellness and wholeness. You are totally aware and infused with your illuminated Magnificence! The abundance of love is streaming in and out in a perfect Figure 8 with all that surrounds you and is within you. Separation is completely dissolved as you bathe in the totality of Unity Consciousness. There are no longer any programs that diminish your significance, your adequacies, your gifts, your worth or your mission. You experience the exalted joy of being free of time and space constraints and revel in the resulting lighted fuel…rocketing you into the orbit of a new experience of the sacred self. You "become" time/space as you create the beginnings of the momentum found in the creative domain of your true self. Revelations amass from the *Soul Sensory Modality* realm of experiences that open worlds only imagined in the Third Dimension. Can you envision all worries, anxieties, fears and separation-inadequacy themes vanish into the mist of transformative energies? Space-time constraints dissolve as the expansive vistas of the Now inform **all** states of being. Imagine a whoosh of movement from within as old debris fields dissolve, releasing you from the confines of Earth/human restraints. The totality of complete safety envelops your entire experience, delightfully dissolving the frequencies of perilous times and dangerous spaces.

The subtle quantum imbalances in your body-energy system can now be felt without fear, as you joyfully embrace the ability to create wellness and harmony for your own inner and outer healing. Your *realized awareness* has increased most exponentially! It is both delightful and amazing to feel your own creative motion of energy together with the beautiful gifts bestowed upon you from other lifetimes, as well within your soul template for this lifetime. You are never torn in the *in-between stagnant field* of dualistic polarization, for you hold the Unity of All...thus creating the New Reality of 5D Consciousness. In this most elegant and sublime Fifth Dimension, each incarnation is a further unveiling of the wondrous world of Soul Matrix. These revelational epiphanies increase the light, breadth and depth of your matrix, inspiring you towards Source completion.

You will be most happy to know everything in the Fifth Dimension is held in the light, including the darkness of other times and places. Consciousness is so elevated that the divination of your magnificent Soul Gifts become realized and manifest, thus creating the new vistas of this Paradigm shift. The outer world becomes the canvas on which the brushstrokes of the amazing world of your high consciousness are seen and felt...always expanding, always moving, yet embracing a stillness by which all else rests. You know and delicately hold this power, expressing it as easily as you breathe, fully embodying the truth that IS the All of Everything. *Choosing the highest path, the highest reality possible at any one time, is the only road most traveled.* For you understand that the beauteous, most sacred outer world is now in total sync with the inner world of highness, and this is most sublime…in Unity with the One.

This is your destiny…this is your Mission! Know that the struggle for this new birth is paramount. *It is in this toiling endeavor of shifting from the "out-in" to the "in-out," from being created to creating and from diminishment to magnificence that the Fifth Dimension emerges into felt frequencies of wholeness.* You might say that the real bona fide undertaking is simply feeling both the crowded movement of transformation and the expansive exhilaration of 5D breath, all at once. As you discover this most sublime and beauteous, highest fifth dimensional Self, there is only one road, one path without hesitation or doubt. To feel this most magnificent, vibrational experience is to have infinite desire to do nothing else but replenish, restore and rejuvenate High-Heart frequencies. Thus, a multifaceted and multidimensional world is birthed resonating proliferant, arable ground for all living beings to live in a world that is so illuminated it creates the exact fertility necessary for all life in the Universe. Remember, Ascension is the sacred process by which Divine Source expands. As you enter the sacred halls of the Fifth Dimension, you join Source motion…expanding your own Source Spark and procreating new realities of illuminated creations. In the Fifth Dimension, you are truly on, what we call, the *destiny path of divination* where the highest path of Ascended potentialities vibrates with sacred vigilance and free choice.

Chapter 6

The Amazing World of the Soul Matrix
Incarnations, Parallel Lives, Essences and Codes

THE SOUL MATRIX

The Soul Matrix contains the All of You, and Consciousness is the light that permeates this sacred temple of You. Together with Source Awareness, this soul/sole home holds all incarnations, essences, cosmic codes and parallel lives that have been created, manifested and materialized by this lighted Consciousness. You might say, the background of the matrix is Source Spark illumination and the spiritual fabric of the matrix is the All of You from the infinite backdrop of the Cosmic Source Matrix. In the Ascension process, many lives have been created in the *all at once* reality to increase both the quotient of light and the remembrance of sacred designs present in your Soul Matrix. For so many material incarnations, there is no recollection of the soul within, let alone the grand matrix of You-consciousness. Remembering the soul-illuminated home from whence you came is certainly a major mission of this current living incarnation.

As stated earlier in this book, the denser the incarnation, the more difficult it is to remember the truth of your higher lighted-self. Yet when the infinitesimal rays of remembrance break through the thick, outer coating of the incognizant self, rockets of illumination burst into being and ripple far into the Universe. This incarnation is such an opportunity for you to awaken to the *total truth* of You and the home from which you came! *Know that each remembrance, each awakening, echoes and enchants the radiating, resonant ribbon of incandescence in the home world of your Soul Matrix, fueling it towards higher transcendence and the multidimensional realities.*

In the Ascension journey, your total consciousness eventually becomes the Matrix…aware of all lives, all essences and transforming cosmic codes into full metamorphic manifestation magic. You may then choose to house this "wholeness of spirit" in a light body or even a highly evolved material body, but without soul particles becoming separate or disremembered. In the Third Dimension, *remembrance and connection* are the critical movements. In the Fifth Dimension, living in the *totality of Now, propagating High-Heart/Soul frequencies and creating from them* become the movements towards *conscious realized awareness*. In the Sixth Dimension, Soul Matrix *becomes* the heart of you, where *merging and becoming* are the movements. You might say, the many ribbons become one ribbon. In the Seventh Dimension, *you simply are* Soul Matrix…living inside the One ribbon, utilizing this "isness" to create beyond the imagination, ever increasing your merging with the Source Divine Matrix of All. There is stillness in the Seventh Dimension that is most potent and absolute, yet all the while you are dancing with Source Consciousness.

For now, simply pause to remember that you have a soul particle, a ribbon within that is the sacred channel to the Hall of Remembrance, the Home of your Soul Matrix and all that can be discovered therein. Every material incarnation has this inner *soul ribbon,* but there are those incarnations that are lived without recognition of such. It may seem like many on your planet have lost this *soul consciousness* recognition altogether; nonetheless, it seeps through even in the dark of night, as if a hand of light reaches into the very center of the human heart, activating its song to wake with love and peace.

As this materialized life is an Ascension life, you have much in your etheric atmosphere helping you with this connection, this recall, this mission. The truth of who you are as a human species can be seen even when it appears you have lost soul consciousness…but oh, when you have this beautiful soul-light streaming through, it accents and brings out the elegance and artistry of the fabric of that which defines the human species. The good news is that the very core of being human stimulates and moves the soul into Awareness, triggering a cascade of remembrances and essences that dance with your human self. This produces a dynamic flow that propels a world shift…changing the face of the Earth and, thus, fulfilling the Ascension prophecy for your planet. As the soul lights up the human template, the two dance together spawning a New Paradigm, a New World. There is nothing that can stop the High-Heart of the human matrix when it is innervated and propelled by the Soul illumination of cosmic Unity Consciousness. This is what is happening on your planet now. Feel this merging within and pause to waltz in the moonlight, sprouting wings to bring light wherever you go. ♡

There are many sacred designs within a Soul Matrix…some fully lit and spinning, while others are dormant, refueling or anticipating a call to action. Many higher beings observe the human Ascension journey by peering into the Soul Matrix to see how active and bright the world of lighted fractals are. It is "sight" that you have not developed in this lifetime, but can begin to recognize as you sit in quiet consciousness with others and sense the essence of their being. At times you may see their inner light pouring forth…feeling the truth of the many illuminated ribbons activated and waving in the material world of their bodies. Most importantly, can you begin to feel this in yourself? Bring awareness to your third and fourth chakra areas to experience the rising soul in energetic form moving about and prodding your awakening. Begin a sitting practice utilizing the glimmering channel of imagination to vision this illuminated soul channel in the center of your being.

Travel in this ascended diamond light and become your lighted sacred designs. Allow this to be the gateway to the star-temple of your Soul Matrix. Envision your star-temple as simply the *unique* cosmic domain where your Soul Matrix lives. Sit within this temple and feel the "you-magnificence" expand…experience the lighted particles of this temple shower you, welcome you and rejoice in you, for you have come home.

Empower your consciousness to absorb this. Know you are so much more than this material body and entrust this light to instill within you the wisdom of the Cosmos! Then, simply relax and rejuvenate without thought or action, all the while feeling the stillness of your body and the movement of illuminated soul. Know you are of the light…expand this realized awareness and once again let your heart lead the way on your Earth plane. ♡

In this Ascension journey, you will be able to access incarnations containing important cosmic-soul essences created just for this life, this time, this world. Know there is something grand that is happening on your planet; this will spark the birth of the *sacred 5D diamond design* within your matrix. It is the Ascension propellant that will accelerate *Soul Sensory Modalities,* the fifth dimensional self and your cosmic origins. You might say, magic and mystical dynamism will return to Earth transforming all who walk her grounds!

INCARNATIONS

In your language, *transmigration* is a wonderful word that embraces the frequencies of reincarnation. After a life is lived, the soul has the opportunity to "migrate" to another incarnated body. Since the soul or spirit force of the Soul Matrix is infinite, it continues to experience opportunities for revelation, evolution and Ascension. There are numerous transmigrations, each taking a partial light ribbon to materialize into a life form. *As Source desires to see itself through creation and manifested multidimensional realities, so too your unique, singular Soul Matrix desires to see itself in form.* Incarnations are transmigrations in material form that actualize some essence of the matrix…each time merging essences that fulfill a mission, a lesson or a learning to expand the illumination of the matrix. *Incarnations are simply the reflected parts of the whole. Ascension is the path to become the whole.*

A quick note…there is no time/space tracking in the Soul Matrix, for all lives are happening at once in the Now. Yet because you live in a time/space paradigm, it is easier to talk of lives as past or future. It is true, therefore, that you visited many incarnated lives in what you perceive to be your past in order to experience the necessary building blocks for this time Now. Thus, two things have been at work.

First, you are done with the karmic wheel and do not have to learn additional lessons by the same level of dimensional experience. You have had many third dimensional lives to learn enough, to forgive enough, to love enough, to hurt enough, to give and take enough, and this wisdom is evident deep within you. It is time to leap from all of these learnings, as the progression and the expanded spectrum they have created helped you arrive here Now. You have lived many different lives traveling on distinct terrains of being and doing. It is also true that suffering, struggle and difficulties have often been the wisest teachers along the way, although you no longer need these programs as the prodding catalysts to move you towards the way of the light.

It is quite noticeable how difficult it is to let go of the old programs that have helped you get here, not because of their highness of vibration but actually because of their lowness. Look around and you will see that in your world. Although various programs have lifted you here, this does not mean you have to become ensconced in them and form your self-image around them. There is nothing else to forgive… you have made it here. Let go and come alive in the New Paradigm of the 5D! ♡

You have worked hard in all your incarnations…can't you see that in your struggles and density attachments? While addictions and dramas appear easy to be attached to, we see the truth of how difficult it is for a light being to hold on to these densities so that growth may occur! These old, self-identity programs are simply messages of your continued dedication to this Ascension process. Don't mistake your debris fields as evidence of unworthiness when they are, in fact, signs of your absolute insistence of utilizing the condensed, jammed experiences of your 3D realities to spring forth to the freedom that is now right before you!

Take a moment to know that just because you have come in this particular or perhaps peculiar 3D Earth incarnation does not mean you are returning to old timelines, past lives and diminished parallel lives. This is not about old learning…it is about neo-learning. You do not have to remember old karmic circles of learning, but instead to re-remember the Ascended Mission of your Cosmic Self in this life at this time! So think of it this way…if you want to hold the forgetting frequency, apply it to old karmic programs and then direct the remembering frequency towards the new horizon where your 5D self is being birthed! After all, you have not come here to be blinded by such things. You have come here to have the Cosmic Sight of Ascension.

Second, your higher/cosmic self has chosen well these incarnations for, along with 3D experiences and lifetimes, you have had many in the high holy 3D and the 5D realms of other planets and universes. Your Cosmic Self chose this time and this life for you to make the jump in your totality of the Ascension Wheel…partly for your progression and partly for you to be in this service of manifesting the higher spiral of birthing new frequencies into this current configuration of life. Don't you see you were ready before you came here? That is one reason you came here! To begin the Ascension journey on Earth, it is much less about your own karmic wheel of learning and more about your Cosmic Service of Transformative Change. This incarnation has the energy potential for metamorphic transformation within your entire Soul Matrix.

This time, this Earth place is a new revelational incarnation experience…completing the karmic wheel in order to begin the awe-inspiring journey on the Ascension path of Conscious Enlightenment. This will have everlasting effects of lifting your entire Soul Matrix to the next illuminated level of Cosmic Design. Incarnations consisting of the old paradigms, lower frequencies and those no longer in alignment with the ascending soul will dissolve, thus creating a new light quotient for the matrix! This life is *that* big and magnificent! Infinite conscious awareness where remembrance lives in between and within all lives will be one of the effects. There will be full consciousness "in-between" lives, therefore lighting up the avenues for abounding, creative sovereignty. In other words, soul consciousness will be fully in realized Awareness…bringing together and merging with all incarnations, prompting a new understanding of the wisdom therein. And, because there will be such enlivened Awareness, a new co-creative potentiality will be available enabling *you* to birth and manifest new realities of incarnate lives.

The ability to access all soul records in the matrix of the All of You will provide the alchemy for the next dimensional level of incarnate expression. How extraordinary for you to be in the driver's seat and Source Illumination to be the fuel for expansion and higher, multidimensional experiences. Realize this particular incarnation provides a potential gateway to the elevated enhancement of soul consciousness. Stay awake and know this truth, and the winged-path shall be revealed. Revelate (to be in the active state of revelation) with this and feel the movement within. *All is in Cosmic-Earth alignment now for the breakthrough moment of all higher frequencies!* ♡

THE WISPS AND WHISPERS OF INCARNATIONS

Earth Lives

Recognizing and remembering other incarnate lives is analogous to arranging a giant, cosmic puzzle in order to see the whole through the parts. These invisible wisps of other animated times of living are more available than is apparent, but *Soul Sensory Modalities* for such registration are often closed to their reception. As the old thinking paradigm of "only one life lived" is surrendered and dissolved, you immediately open a portal for these impressions and experiences to speak. Once freed from making this life the only life, you create a readiness template for the realization of the other lives. Think about it…when you really believe that this particular life is the only life, the pressure to make it the right life simply makes it too great to actually live life. You are not here to make this the perfect and only life, but rather you are here in this life to add to the transcendence of your Soul Matrix. Believing and knowing the truth of the many lives manifested by your soul consciousness is most crucial in opening the doorway to subtle cues and clues.

It is easier to feel the whispers from a previous Earth life because you often move in places and times that hold the record of past life frequencies. For instance, déjà vu moments are "flash-occasions" when you experience familiar recognitions of some vibratory field of past knowing chronicled in the Akashic records. These are "bleed-throughs" of a frequency seepage or infiltration from the time/space continuum and should be treated with sacred confidence of the truth of the world of soul-reincarnation. If these moments could be catalogued over time, you might be able to piece together the whole of some other life lived. In those déjà vu moments, it might be quite surprising to know you may actually travel (in the blink of an eye) to that life on the slipstream of the familiar frequency band. The stronger the déjà vu experience, the more likely you journeyed in the interdimensional slipstream of the Soul Matrix and experienced a real time moment from another lifetime. These time/space warps happen so instantaneously that they barely register in the 3D consciousness, and you are simply left with the familiar feeling of being there before!

Dreamtime

Memories of past lives come in many mysterious clues and cues. Often, they arrive in the whimsical dreamtime, when outside shades are closed and the inside channels are opened to the realm of Soul Matrix remembrance. Particular repetitive themes, such as places you have never been and landscapes never seen, may appear to have little connection to this current life but come in familiar shapes in the terrain of remembrance. Perhaps people continually arrive that you can't place in your current life, yet there is an inexplicable intimacy with them in your dreamtime. Themes, places, people and events may all be messages from another incarnate part of your higher consciousness... delivering the light in the dark of the night to bring remembrance, restoration and rejuvenation. Pause with these dreamtime soul-ribbons and you might begin to intuit and feel the life beyond the current you!

Awake-Time

In waking life, you may be particularly attracted to or know information about a specific place and/or time of Earth history that you have not yet garnered from this lifetime. Perhaps you feel a certain mystical calling towards some occupation, skill or artistry. Propensities and attractions often are "bleed-throughs" from other lives. To think that all of your choices, skills, assets, desires come from this one template is putting a lot of emphasis on one small lifetime!

Follow these wispy strands of evidential truth, for they are the lost parts of you that create revelations of great importance for this mission, this lifetime. As you move along in this human life, feel those faint whispers that say, "I have been here before, or I have done this before." Can you begin to pursue these incarnate adventures with the verve and gusto that you pursue your own life? Visit your libraries of gathered books and let the reserved pages call to you as you wander through the vast volumes of written words. Look at a globe and the charted maps of your world to see what moves you to peer closer and allow discovery of some new yet familiar place. Take some unexplored route along the highways of your life...often the road less traveled is the passageway towards invisible landscapes.

Remember, your sensory perceptual modalities are not only physical antennas but *soul-receivers* as well, extracting and distilling unrealized information from another place and time. Smell an aroma, touch some material, see a landscape, hear the song that ignites a faint knowing within...a deep remembrance not quite placed in this life. Know these are "bleed-throughs" whispering to you from the deep space of your Soul Matrix of other lives and other times. If you bring this consciousness, this realized awareness, to these sensory "incidents," you will widen the channel for more luminous and salient information regarding these transmigrations. After all, if you do not know the truth that these lie within your own dimension, you will never be able to know from whence they came! Follow the breath of other lives that surround you, pursue the pieces of this grand puzzle and never doubt your intuitive stirrings about these migratory soul events. *This isn't you creating that which does not exist; it is you beginning to see and feel that which has already come to be.* Your eternal consciousness is alive and well in so many material manifestations. Seek them and you will begin to know the magnificence of your Soul Matrix that lives here…now!

As you travel on these migratory expeditions of consciousness, seek and behold those other incarnate lives where aspirations for higher frequency living appear and resonate with the Ascension path. This is far more important than past incarnate expeditions that quench the thirst for further debris fields of past injuries, traumas or egoistic importance. You have lived many lives that have prepared you for this most magnificent life…listen carefully and they will convey ancient and future truths fueling you to become the All that you are in this life.
♡

Off-Planet Lives

It is important to know that Light warriors and Ascension journeyers have had many more off-planet lives than Earth migrations, and it is difficult to procure the subtle and fragrant soul frequencies of off-planet lives. Isn't it most interesting that you must first accept the existence of such off-planet civilizations before you can know you have been part of those civilizations? Perhaps this is a subtle or not so subtle means of unveiling the disclosure process. In a manner of thinking, it challenges your Earth-centric views and eases the fear by which you might imagine off-planet life…especially if you identify with having one of those lives! For many, once an incarnation where the color of your skin was blue and hairless and your eyes the beautiful changing shades of the cosmic sky is recognized and envisioned, different cosmic races in peculiar and astonishing new places will open to you. To know this brings you closer to the miraculous and breathtaking expression of creative Source.

Remember, your wisdom of all lives is more limitless in soul consciousness between lives and through free will you choose assignments in the far-reaching star paradigms of the Universe. This is the Ascension path. Some of you already feel strange in the human body and occasionally see yourself quite differently through random glances in your reflective surfaces. Begin to peruse the volumes of images your artists have painted of faraway places and stranger-still faces. You might begin to gaze in familiar ways on some other body housing some other life. Off-planet lives hold enormous information about this particular incarnation on Earth and the mission therein.

CONNECTING TO THOSE WHO HONOR THIS LIFE

In this very moment of Now, there are living incarnations of your illumined soul beckoning you with their unparalleled and unique ribbons of manifestation. These incarnated streamers of siphoned consciousness are aware of you in this life…on this Earth…right Now. They are living, developing tools and creating essences of soul material relevant and momentous to your life now. Fantastical? Yes! For many, it may be unimaginable that other current incarnate lives relevant to your soul transcendence are happening now.

As you begin to accept and uncover this *cosmic truth*, you will have access to the most accelerating manifestation propellant to enhance the embodiment of your unique cosmic/soul-skills. To know these lives is to recognize a deep-seated part of you, for these lives exist within you and surround you. This cannot be understood through the mental highways of your 3D thinking apparatus, as travel-ways for such communication only exist in the fifth dimensional realm. It is also important to realize that tools and essences coming from these other lives require you to be online in higher frequencies beyond that of the 3D. So these incarnations, let's call them Advanced Cosmic Entities (ACE), have both the remembrance of their designed mission and immense consciousness of spirit to reach you through the invisible threads of the Cosmic Byway. Think about it…you actually have these Advanced Cosmic Entities (ACE) here to nourish, facilitate and bolster your transformational journey through frequency downloads of the no-time and no-space cosmic waves in the ethers.

You will not "understand" this at first, but you may be able to feel it! The Advanced Cosmic Entities (ACE) are sending cosmic attunements that will enable you to upload these essences and tools, as well as open receptor sites to house the new cosmic light waves coming into your planet. However, it is impossible to hold these experiences within your 3D mind because this incoming cosmic-data is resonant and aligned with the human High-Heart. Certain of your "aha" moments are actually these communications! In fact, there are times when you grasp elements of cosmic understanding which then begin to transform your worldview and mission motivation. Perhaps suddenly, realized artistic and creative propensities burst within you, entering with a beautiful salutation from the deep recesses of your core essence. These cosmic communications from your ACE light up your *star DNA* causing a metamorphic, alchemic experience within the deep realms of your body.

These Advanced Cosmic Entities (ACE) not only have detailed knowledge of you here on Earth (after all they are birthed from the same Soul Matrix) but are intricately involved in anointing you with the fibers of life spirit that will enhance and upgrade your mission potentialities. Of course, free will is paramount in your decision to acknowledge and incorporate these beautiful life soul-materials. If you question your magnificence, Now is the time to put that question to rest! As you step into your magnificent frequency template, you will open channels for communication and reception. If you have been working with guides, most likely one of them is such an ACE. It is you in different form and function, but nevertheless a part of your quite amazing Soul Matrix.

The question becomes...how might you recognize this? First, begin to hold the truth that such an ACE incarnation exists simultaneous to your current human life and is solely (souly) relevant in its mission to enhance your life on Earth...Now. Compose an invitation to your ACE and envision the response. Make sure you put an RSVP on the invite, for that provides a heart link to where you live! Then unfurl imagined channels to this advanced life and allow your receiver ports to be lit up. Invite, expand recognition portals and feel the movement of the transmigratory action of receiving upgrades and astonishing, unexpected wisdom of cosmic proportions. Know that you have human coaches or specialists on your planet that can also help with these connections, especially those who engage in, what you call, Quantum Healing Hypnotic Techniques or past life regressions. In these processes, it is important that the intention is to connect with these "higher incarnate lives" rather than the old, posted roads of past traumas and dilemmas. Of course, clearing these debris fields is beneficial and important, although receiving the inspiring connection and opening channels to your beautiful, higher lives-lived can shed exponentially more light on your current mission, soul manifestation and Ascension journey. Quiet the mind, open your **High-Heart** and plan to be surprised by the blessed reunion of the most beautiful incarnations of your Soul Matrix! ♡

NEW TIMELINES AND TEMPLATES

As you open channels to these life templates, the Soul Matrix network expands. Thus, you set the pace for not only your 5D manifested life but future lives moving towards 6D fulfillment and Soul Matrix awareness.

This life is a "breakthrough" life...in other words, a life that is dimensionally transcending from 3D to 5D. There will be a time when you live in the totality of 5D and have total remembrance of the cosmic mechanics of this soul quantum leaping, thus giving access to the breakthrough energetics necessary for multidimensional travel into the Sixth Dimension! Know that when this happens you will have access to all lives and relevant energies. You will not necessarily remember the lives per se, rather the energy templates of those lives and their relevance to the journey towards Soul Matrix completion.

Indeed…this particular life is quite momentous and far-reaching! As you make this elevated leap, a lighted, spirited wave of illuminated energy will be generated that will spark your entire Soul Matrix into a higher level of multidimensional awareness. After all, the Ascension path is not only to bring the New Dawn era to Earth but the New Dawn to your Soul Matrix, thus providing the cosmic fuel for more Ascension advancement. You see, on Earth you have the extraordinary opportunity to ascend from the shadowing of spirit to the dawning of the soul light. This 5D transformational journey enables your entire Soul Matrix to elevate to a higher sacred design where pure Source Sound frequencies emanate, making possible eventual Source merging in the higher planes of multidimensional consciousness. The consciousness of spirit that this produces transmutes all free will decisions from then on. Learning no longer takes place with the lessons of the dark, rather in classrooms of the light.

Take a moment to imagine that your only task or mission is generating and accelerating the light quotient of the Soul Matrix so that more lives-lived are in the process of the Ascended multidimensional journey. It is no wonder that you have a cooperative of other incarnate lives invested in your process in this life you live! This creates quite a cosmic event as it produces a light wave in the Universe that expands the power of the Breath of Source Light. As you expand, so too does the Universe, and in this dynamic, mystical process you commove and galvanize the potentiality of birthing new Universes. You see, what happens in the Micro life has enormous impact on the Macro living soul. After all, the Micro moves and forms the Macro as the Macro moves and forms the Micro…all at once. What an intense dance of the Universe…the ultimate Sacred Figure 8! Unity in every part and every part in the Whole.

You are preparing essences, codes and maps in this lifetime for other lifetimes to come! How incredible! You might want to ponder what creations to manifest in this lifetime, for whatever you embody now becomes the inherited blueprint for future lives and the Soul Light of the Universe. There are cosmic libraries that actually store the immense and endless ribbons of soul manifestations of each Soul Matrix. Although impossible to conceptualize, it is quite wondrous to simply realize its existence. On our craft, we are able to replicate and store copies of your own ascending template so that other lives on other planets can benefit and learn from your amazing journey. We knew you before this incarnation…remember? We are guardians for your journey…savoring the flowering beauty of your ever-evolving consciousness and knowing that the illuminated ripples of your light are already changing the Universe in which we all live. ♡

PARALLEL LIVES

Every turn, every choice, every crossroad and every potentiality is held and exits within the Universal Field. It is not easy to comprehend that all choice points you have had in this lifetime are "unrealized" realities in other slipstreams of this same incarnation of you. *When you actualize a choice point, you transform an embryonic potentiality into a manifested reality where consciousness or realized awareness consequentially resides.* In that respect, you have had, and continue to have, many parallel lives. It is important to note that the particular "realized" parallel life that is currently experienced continues to be filled with choice points that birth potentialities into realized realities. Every choice produces a powerful awakening that bursts into phenomenal perceptibility of the self in action. This then becomes the home where your consciousness resides.

Now, it seems a common experience in this particular incarnation to feel as though you have lived numerous lifetimes. Those various, experiential "lifetimes" are examples of *parallel timeline jumping*. The particular slipstream you live in depends on the *consciousness light quotient.* As consciousness becomes more evolved, one's volition moves towards and resonates with higher vibrational templates, crystalizing the Ascension path. I tell you this…you have already jumped many parallel life timelines, as you have chosen your current life's destiny of higher consciousness, fifth dimensional transformation. Your consciousness has aspired to a new more whole, more fully realized awareness and, in that moment, you experience and bring into manifestation a timeline jump. Every higher frequency you feel builds a quotient for jumping timelines into a higher parallel life in this incarnation. As you live more fully in higher aspirations and intentions, the quotient of lighted energy propagates a new timeline…of your evolving consciousness.

Often, there may be only vague recollections of preceding timelines and the further back they go the more foreign they may feel. If the seeds of change have not fully opened to endow consciousness with enough buoyancy and stability to stay adrift in the new life, it will be easy to be uprooted, landing once again in more recent, albeit denser, timelines. Indeed, there will be more sinking and slippage in the initial stages of the new parallel life. As you begin to live in a lighter, energetic, parallel matrix, old triggers, clues and trapdoors can still appear, rushing you headlong back to old patterns, habits and denser configurations of older timelines. Then, when behaviors, thoughts and feelings align with that particular "past" parallel life, you simply return to it. This is certainly part of the weaving process. As remarkable progress is made in 5D self-manifestation, just as rapidly the fall into the abyss of old paradigms can be sobering and depleting.

It is important at each life jump to sever the tethers of old, phenomenal living-patterns in those past places. In one magical moment, the manifestation of these realized-realities come into being and you are replete with global insights, cosmic wisdom and high-heart energies, thus actualizing a significant timeline jump. Yet, at first glance, these moments may seem fleeting and temporary as it is most easy to return to more slumbering states of being. However, each time you experience this, you pave wider and deeper channels for this timeline jump to become more accessible and manifest. Eventually, you become "new and improved." You and others may take notice of something "different" and more beautiful about you. Remember, the direction of timeline jumping is a two-way street and so, without conscious attunement, slipping into the abyss of the past can easily be accomplished by falling into old habits of perception, feeling and thinking.

On the Ascension journey, there are many lifetimes experienced in one incarnation through the process of parallel timeline jumping. Haven't you noticed that what, how or who you were ten years ago no longer fits with what you feel today? Moving towards your highest parallel life is one description of Ascension! Remember, just as incarnations embedded in karmic wheel material are dissolving, dispersing and releasing energy from your Soul Matrix, so too are denser, debris-laden parallel lives deliquescing and fading from awareness. More recent parallel lives can certainly come to bear on your future choices as you have slight recollections of old habits and attachments. Solidifying the new "higher-frequency life" can be done through imprinting and laying the new grid with these higher consciousness experiences so that neo-memories and the new circuitry can establish redesigned habits and practices.

Humans may indeed be unconscious of their highest parallel life and so have not been inspired to make those "high-frequency" choice points. Rest assured you are making the material for this *right now*. You are spinning with higher frequency propagations and opening gateways to these new choice points where you will continue to choose lighter behaviors, thoughts, feelings and manifestations for your inner and outer world. As you become more conscious of these, you provide portals for timeline jumping. Once the leap is made, your consciousness becomes the embodiment of this new, higher-realized awareness, thus allowing the feeling you have lived many lives in just this one life to stream forth!

The most ascended life in this current incarnation awaits you and is your destiny, if you so choose. Every choice point that comes up on your consciousness screen is an opportunity to opt for the highest vibrational field of being you. Learning to dissolve old pathways of thinking and feeling frees you for flight into new timelines and higher parallel lives in new time/space zones of living. Learning to hold and manifest High-Heart choices within your consciousness is the path towards timeline jumping within this incarnate you. As you become more conscious of these potentialities, this by itself produces a more manifest highway system of roads that become the natural choice point for future travel.

Timeline jumping is the ability to open energetic-receptor sites for receiving light information that informs conscious choice (free will) towards higher frequency domains of living. Every breakthrough 5D frequency that is felt builds the light-quotient for jumping timelines towards the completion of your Ascension journey in this life. Of course, this is simultaneously happening to your beautiful Earth planet as well. You might say, you are walking hand in hand with the evolving life on Earth all the while becoming the New Paradigm of Unity and Love. *In this process, the event horizon of the new Ascension crossing occurs, moving through the boundaries of time/space 3D permanency and entering the permeable realm of the ever-being and ever-transforming Fifth Dimension.*

So you see, you just might want to become more conscious parallel timeline jumpers! Allow your day to be filled with High-Heart endeavors, such as acts of kindness, service and compassion. Can you stay consistent enough in these aspirations to witness, experience and manifest these illuminated frequency templates in your current reality? Consistently and persistently pursuing "realized-awareness" creates the fuel for leaping towards a lighter, brighter parallel life. Take a moment to identify High-Heart frequencies and then infuse them into actions, thoughts and body awareness throughout the day. This creates harmonic convergence towards an illuminated parallel life.

Watch what transforms before your eyes: diet, people, assets, desires, skills, jobs, service, communities and family, to name but a few.

With each leap, you will gravitate towards an external reality that matches your new, higher-vibe, energetic matrix that provides stabilization and resonation with this advanced version of your life. Remember to bring beautiful realized experiences and wisdom from previous parallel lives, for it is not about abandoning past things but rather bringing forward conscious material that resonates with the Ascension journey. You are a soul architectural-template in process! *As you move with more certitude and assuredness in managing free will consciousness in the infinite field of potentialities becoming manifest, you will help the world stay steady in its own courageous timeline leap.* And, as you gather momentum with fellow human travelers, you will accelerate the Transformation for the New Lighted Age on your entire planet. As Earth moves to her highest parallel life in her current incarnation, it indeed stimulates other planets for the same resonant movement! Thus, the Golden Figure 8 is in sacred movement, ever-expanding the Universal Source Energy into the transformative dance of birth and renewal.

As you bring consciousness to your parallel lives and timeline jumping, time itself changes...sometimes slowing almost to a complete halt and other times speeding up to enormous velocities. Jumps in consciousness also cause the space around you to look differently. As you move to higher parallel lives, you actually are in a new frequency domain and these smaller changes eventually lead to dimensional shifts from the Third Dimension to the Fifth Dimension. Time becomes more fluid and moveable as consciousness becomes the sculptor of time and space. When there is a realization that you are not stuck in time and space but rather dancing in the Universe of frequencies, realized-awareness of *frequency living* is fruited and bloomed. Nothing is fixed as nothing is permanent, and in this you have freedom of choice. You are the creator of the realities of your vibrational states and as such can move out of the previous place of being into the new *placeless-state* of being. In so doing, you shift perspective from outside permanency to inside flexibility and ever-moving frequency experiences. What is permanent is the constancy of movement rather than the fixed position of motionless being.

In the eternal dance of cosmic frequency living, there is a sense that this is what indeed is the "always and forever." Movement is guaranteed when there is a realization that you are the one creating that movement. After all, you are changing constantly…even your body tells you this. *It is time for you to realize that your creative consciousness is the grand master alchemist for your own metamorphic Self-Revolution.* When this happens, it is most easy to timeline jump to a more illuminated parallel life. After all, Ascension is the transcendent process of moving towards the highest consciousness of your current incarnate being, thus bringing the potentiality of your 5D self into manifested reality!

It is not as hard as it seems, having done this already so many times while seeking the highest part of the path. Simply do not lose awareness of every moment! Keep steady in the Now, for this is where consciousness resides. In addition, the Now is the only frequency that produces the fertile launching field of timeline jumping. Stay Conscious, flow in the Now, embrace the illuminated frequency manifestations and you will become the advanced template of the New Human! Listen to the whispers of the lighted-traces left in the higher realms by your Soul Matrix…you will then know from whence you came and where you are meant to be.

Ascension is a process that is always in motion and this very motion of life moves one into more realized awareness. This awareness bears witness to your free will choices to continue on the higher path, thus bringing consciousness to the motion of Ascended Awareness. When you came into this life, you carried with you the alchemic, alive template of pyramidal parallel lives…so that the highest potentiality might become manifest in this reality at this time in this current transmigration! Utilizing the Source power of free will to bring 5D potentialities into *realized-realities* is indeed manifesting the highest parallel reality of this incarnation. This, my friends, is the magic of the Ascension journey!

ESSENCES AND COSMIC CODES

ILLUMINATED SOUL ESSENCES

Soul essences of your higher potentialities live within you. These essences are the material substance of your soul incarnations... the quintessence of the purest numinous material for the Ascension process. They are cosmic kernels of fuel that lie dormant waiting for consciousness to call for the awakening and unfurling of these potentialities into manifesting realities. Activated, distilled soul tinctures or concentrates unleash specific gifts, skills, assets, powers and magic to be utilized in one's consciousness journey.

Inspired essences are the creative material of the sculptor's hand, the artist's brush and spirit's soaring. It is time to allow these inherent, star-seeded essences to consummate fully, thus offering a wellspring of magic, mystic revelation and sacred gifts of soul manifestation within the incarnated self. Have you noticed that certain creative and metaphysical endeavors only came to fruition within you in recent years? Perhaps some creative talent (art, music, movement, etc.) or spiritual activation floods consciousness and begins to materialize, only after spending a lifetime without expression or even awareness that this is part of mission manifestation. *As the old paradigm programs release, expansive allowance of time/space movement provides a birthing dock for these essences to come forth.*

If you believe you do not contain soul essences within because you have never been told they exist, it is easier to assume the old stories about your lack therein. Your mission is to unlock that which you brought with you for this time on Earth! There is currently a vibrational, illuminated template encircling Earth that softly intimates these truths in the wee hours of the night or the pausing moments of the day. Listen carefully and move past the gated regions within that hold the old ideas of self. Instead, cross into the unknown, mysterious territory of your inner core that has been carefully, gently cradling and encircling these soul essences for this time Now. These are the remedies for all that ails you…for within, you have been the keeper of curative metamorphic and transforming frequency fields for birthing the 5D self you have come to be. Let these essences break free and feel the truth of the All of You. After all, you brought them here! Perhaps, now you can see how magnificent the vision of your higher soul consciousness is, for it "knew" what you would need for this incredible mission on Earth and so provided, within your deep quantum templates, these essences. ♡

COSMIC CODES

The Sacred Figure 8 Transfiguration

Soul essences are the spiritual material of transformation, and cosmic codes illuminate and unlock pathways for soul material manifestation. As illuminated soul essences manifest or come to be, a certain light code is released that triggers cosmic codes into activation. Receptor sites are then opened and expanded for the incoming "outer space" Cosmic Codes. Are you ready?

Cosmic Codes are triggered by both the process of essence manifestation and downloads from above. Manifesting soul essences make capable the tolerance for cosmic code activations. The Sacred Figure 8 of transfiguration is triggered whereby the essences affect the codes and the codes in turn affect the essences; therefore, cosmic codes have the potential to unlock additional essences within and bring them to fruition. Each brings to the other a synchronistic frequency template to increase the opportunity for transformation and revelation.

Many in the human race are currently unlocking 5D essences for the Ascension process since their higher consciousness is now coming online and in focus. As a result, this produces more landing fields for incoming illuminated wisdom from the Cosmos. This cosmic light triggers DNA changes that then open cosmic-encrypted DNA sequence codes or keys within the body, and within these DNA activations additional soul essences are released and abound. It is the reason so many are increasing their ability to activate their *Soul Sensory Modalities (SSM)*. There are essences within you that hold the template for all *Soul Sensory Modalities.* Activation is the key!

Imprinted Keys of Memory Revelation

Encrypted keys can awaken memories (which are themselves hidden essences of imprinted keys of remembrance) releasing deeper truths of this mission and your connection to the Cosmos. Think of it this way...you have a star-studded treasure chest within and these sacred, alive codes contain the exact encryption to open 5D frequency libraries. Cosmic Codes are keys to setting free the contents within, including imprinted keys of other incarnations, parallel lives and current bilocation experiences. *Remember, you have many more stored remembrances (imprinted keys of higher conscious experiences) than you do of the indentations from this particular incarnated life experience.*

Through cosmic code activation, you are opening to a whole wondrous world of invisible phenomenon taking shape in your current time/space reality! As you bring vision to those sacred shapes and contours, you will see the truth of who you are and whence you have come! You will also have invisible experiences (with more becoming tangible and seen) in the higher realm of your 5D self. By way of bilocation of consciousness, you will go to many places at night through the transportation system of your *Soul Sensory Modalities* where glimpses of other realms, dimensions and timelines are seen.

And so, you already have knowledge of these superimposed realities and experiences. As you move up the ladder towards higher 5D, you will also have more access to *remembering* these fifth dimensional experiences and travels. You will be able to access nighttime corridors and "other-worldly" waking moments where your 5D self stores "imprint keys" of the lighted contours and sacred shapes of the New Dawn experiential phenomenon. You will begin to know how to travel interdimensionally and intrapsychically because you will be able to access imprint keys or memories that have been frequently happening in your 5D world, albeit unbeknownst to your 3D consciousness.

The 5D self is very aware of all experiences and the frequencies held therein, including the total mastery of *SSM*. However, you are in a weaving dance with the different dimensions and so do not have total access to this higher 5D consciousness, nor to the memories of being there. Hypothetically speaking, let's say there is a scale of 1-5 where 1 is total 3D cognizance and 5 is total 5D awareness. As you reach slightly above 3, a channel opens between where you are now and the totality of your 5D self and, through this channel, key imprints or memories of the experiences of your 5D self are accessible and clear. These "imprint keys" have been sent to you through these channels so that you might see what your higher self has been and is up to. When located on levels 1 and 2, you simply do not have the receptor ports to "read" these imprinted "documents." As consciousness expands, there will be a realization that you have indeed been busy seeing, hearing, doing, feeling and knowing more things than have been made apparent by your 3D incarnate self.

How exciting to begin to peer into the mysterious and wondrous life of your higher self! And as you do, the merging with that vibrational field will become more effortless and potent. *The very movement into higher consciousness configurations creates the keys to unlocking even more soul essences and cosmic codes within. This then IS the Path of Ascension.* Know you are here to be in this most wondrous activation of frequency alignment in the fifth dimensional world.

Star Portals and the Inner Landing Fields

Encrypted, cosmic star-codes are capable of building star portals and landing fields within the bio/mental/emotional and spiritual bodies, thus preparing humans for the enormous incoming Source Light that is illuminated with cosmic wisdom and healing. This is all preparation for the flight of Ascension-Activation that is happening on the planet Now. As the planetary beings on Earth have so dramatically increased their consciousness quotient, there is an improved toleration for this very intense and potent cosmic frequency alignment. *Through soul essence activation and code-mapping of new gateways, receptor sites and imprint keys, the circuitry expansion of 5D consciousness is blooming in its metamorphic travels from a 3D human incarnate to a 5D high consciousness being in human uniform…all at once bringing Unity Consciousness into full fruition.*

ACTIVATION: THE ALCHEMIC DANCE OF ATTUNEMENT AND INTEGRATION

Having *realized awareness* that you have "carried-forward" these soul essences and cosmic codes is the first part; the activation phase is perhaps a bit more mysterious. For, what good is a dormant fuel without activation and eventual materialization? The awakening of these star essences and cosmic codes can occur through many means.

Simply Being the Highest Frequency Template

The very act of aspiring towards the highest potentiality for this particular life stirs consciousness towards lighting those hidden avenues where these illuminated gems reside. *The long-awaited presence (presents) of these coded soul essences will be unlocked and realized simply by experiencing and becoming infused with High-Heart frequencies.* Vibrating with these fifth dimensional frequencies provides a catalytic condition within that releases these soul treasures. Isn't it a magnificent prescript that naturally being in the quivering resonance of your 5D self energizes and activates these miracle essences for further enacting your mission as a fifth dimensional Self? *The holy geometric Sacred Figure 8 is once again in universal harmonic convergence…as the very cosmic nature of the 5D self anoints, propels and magnifies the exact frequency soul essences to further ignite the very mission of the fifth dimensional Self.* Both the frequencies of the 5D being and frequency activations inspired therein are working in total synchronistic movement to bring illumination and manifestation to the Ascension process.

As you experience your High-Heart vibrational field, feel the spiraling essences awaken and hear their living breath intimate what is to come. Explore these blooming soul essences and let them become your new guideposts for further adventure! Remember, you are traveling in the invisible realm of all possibilities and, therefore, old maps of moving forward cannot trace a path in the new dimensional planes. *Let the knowing of the unknown be your guide. You are a New Human… creating new passageways to the cosmic maps currently unfolding on this beautiful 5D Earth plane.*

Incarnations Creating Essences and Codes for Ascension

As discussed above, there are "current" preeminent incarnations generating specific essences for this Ascension process you are now experiencing on Earth. It is paramount to identify and connect with these soul transmigrations because they are particularly relevant and pivotal for this life. Opening to these beautiful beings (all part of your Soul Matrix) who have prescribed lives not only offer lighted-fuel for this journey but also activate particular gifts of potent spiritual wisdom and magical power. This increases your ability to turn on your *SSM* and accentuate your capacity to travel the etheric airwaves of the Synchronistic Web. Again, you will not find formulas in current paradigms of the 3D world for downloading this…for the very act of understanding and connecting with this migratory light-fuel expands the current paradigm and births a new wisdom school of dilatant transformation. *Feel the incarnate lives that are pulsing the rhythmic kiss of these starlit jewels so they may illuminate this path with the glimmer of what is to come!*

Higher Parallel Lives Creating Illuminated Buoyancy

There are also higher parallel lives where these essences have become part of your bio, mental, emotional and spiritual templates. Visioning these higher lives, daring to go beyond to see the highest version of you, will help you "see" these soul essences in full manifestation. You might want to ask, "What would I need in *this* life to accelerate and manifest my Ascension path in order to live in a fifth dimensional reality, and what powers or skills, frequency templates and fulfillment promises would be in total synchronistic alignment with my 5D self and what I am here to do?" Realize when you put this list together, it means you have already peered into your higher parallel life experiences and have seen the truth of who and what you can be. Now…take a leap into that very higher life, activating the soul essences that are already moving through another time/space paradigm! This timeline jump can happen in one moment of revelational consciousness.

Live Theater: Guides and the Ascended Ones

Live theater…where consciousness becomes the stage and the metaphysical/spiritual players influencing and guiding life are more easily seen. Certainly, the whispers of higher guides can be heard when consciousness is stilled and the movement of the celestial winds glide slowly into momentary awareness. There are so many guides spiraling through the flowering etheric fields of your raised potentialities. They kiss you with grace, transmuting lower energies and birthing new paths for exploration and dance. Sometimes you can feel them gently touching your mind field, lighting up the hidden corridors where these magical soul-lit essences wait to be bathed by the awakening sustenance of conscious awareness. These guides may come from your Earth ancestral line of wisdom keepers, or from the angelic realm where the soft petals of diamond light abound.

There are also many extraterrestrials that have come to assist you so that you might soon join the New Cosmic Neighborhood. Remember, free will always drives the process of transformation of consciousness… for it is this conscious-intention that opens these sacred gates to the guides beyond. As these ancestral, celestial and extraterrestrial guides see your 5D abilities, soul essences and heightened consciousness coming to life, they can further aid in this most magical unfolding miracle of Ascension. They are with you, my friends…watching and waiting for opportunities to download and upgrade your template of higher learning. Heed their presence. At the very least, you will come to understand and embrace the abundant elixir of experiencing these beautiful beings in the invisible realm, thereby making visible that which has been unknown. And in that knowing, you will hover for an eternal moment in your own magnificence…for it is that magnificent radiating frequency that called them to you! Know, as well, that the pages of this book are here as guides because you have called them to be. ♡

Illuminated Gifts from the Cosmos

The sacred flight of the Diamond Light is coming into the Earth plane now from many Sources. Remember, diamond light is the radiating illumination from the fifth dimensional Sacred Domain. There is a divine portal that has opened from the Galactic Sun that is now allowing Divine Source Light to shower Earth and her inhabitants with the powers of Cosmic Essences. You might call these Cosmic Essences more generalized illuminative forces that are given to planetary inhabitants in order to magnify and multiply the potentiality of essence manifestation. There were also major astronomical events in 2020, such as the NeoWise comet and the Jupiter/Saturn conjunction, as well as lunar and solar eclipses that continue to open pivotal stargates. These cosmic apertures allow enormous light to enter Earth's atmosphere, bringing prodigious informational and alchemic downloads to humans. These downloads often include catalysts for unlocking these miraculous essences within, as well as bringing new Cosmic Codes to the human species. So you see, as humans begin to increase their light quotient, inner portals open to receive, absorb and digest these higher cosmic vibrational codes. Rest assured that these amazing Cosmic Happenings would not be occurring if the impenetrable shields of old, human paradigms were in full guard of the stagnant, static state of 3D Earth. Transformation of consciousness is indeed fueling and charging these once-decaying grounds with higher vibrational fields of bloom and blossom!

Earth Sites

Ancient, soul-planetary essences and Earth codes are also opening around your planet...offering the human species planted sustenance that will aid in this ever-thriving Ascension process. Again we see the transfiguration of the Sacred Figure 8, for as the sacred essences are opened within you, they have an activating effect on those planetary Earth codes. Some imprint keys/codes are Earth-created and some have been buried by indigenous cultures of planet Earth, while others have been placed here by off-planet cosmic civilizations desiring to be of service to your planet. In fact, some codes have been waiting for millions of years to be released. There are also imprinted cosmic codes left behind by cultures not written about in your history books, including the Atlanteans, Lemurians and hybrid human/ET cultures. These civilizations on Earth were highly conscious of the 5D metamorphic time of Now and left coded messages to be unfurled at just this time.

As humans evolve into their true 5D soul essence and resonate this high consciousness frequency, it will create a rippling effect that calls out via telepathic radar, "We are here, open and ready for the Earth to release these coded messages of what is to come." Some ancient Earth cultures were able to advance to fully manifest 5D communities and still can be found on Earth, as in the "mythical" Shambhala and several other most-astonishing light communities. They are here to guide and fuel this process on Earth and stabilize their beautiful, manifested reality that will enable the current potentialities to navigate the crossing point of consciousness to the New Dawn ahead. As these mysterious, sacred messages are being released, new memories of Earth's history will be recalled, and the expansion from such memory retrieval will be most stunning and amazing. And, as these beautiful Earth/Cosmic Codes are available for your transformation, the rippling effect will be extraordinary, allowing the human race to achieve and maintain stability in 5D consciousness! Once again, we have the Golden Sacred Figure 8 of Earth and human transfiguration through synchronistic time/space openings of a most majestic experience. These codes will be both reparative and transformational, as they will heal that which ails the Earth herself and transform the etheric terrain so that humans will be lifted in a manner where the Above and Below will be merged into complete harmony and Unity.

The amazing purification resulting from these new 5D essences, elixirs and keys will also open star portals to other cosmic civilizations, thus producing more interplanetary communication and travel. This will inspire and make possible new modalities of healing, living, wellness-consciousness and harmonious Sacred Unity. In turn, Earth will begin to shine its light outwards, no longer being in a confinement modality where inner turmoil and geocentric thinking are center stage. Finally, to take one's place among the stars...bringing light to the All of One and to the One of All! It is a marvelous event...perhaps now you can see why there are so many of us here! We are present in a Circle of Light surrounding your planet, assembled from so many places and times in the Cosmos. There are celestials, ancestral and extraterrestrials already celebrating the turning of the Sun, and that Sun is your Earth becoming the Light.

So, dear ones, take time to sit with the truth of the totality of your Soul Matrix, the cherished living temple of your incarnations, parallel lives, essences and cosmic codes. Sit with these most wondrous messages and birth the eternal moment of Now. The frequencies of these words on this page are star-codes opening some forgotten corridor within you, bringing you closer to the Magnificence of You. Know this truth and step into the invisible world, making it apparent and perceptible for this new dimensional consciousness. You have such amazing co-creative forces within. This is how Source works...giving and placing the beauteous codes of Lighted Knowledge within each spark of Life so that *As Above So Below* movement of illumination can begin to materialize, thus expanding Source Spark throughout the Universe. So be it and so it is! ♡

Chapter 7

Tools for Ascension

How wonderful to be in the flow of the 5D frequency domain simply by utilizing the very tools for Ascension to access the Fifth Dimension! Tools and practices are the path, yet the tools for Ascension will not be found in the 3D world. And so it is truly not the journey's end, but the act of praxis, methods and manners producing frequency states of being...and once there, you have arrived. These formulary blueprints invite frequency states of being, thus creating an experience within. The vibratory state of the experience itself creates realities! The tool is simply a vehicle for the Ascending experience. The experience happens within this vehicle and so the destination is found in the utilization of the blueprint mechanisms themselves!

Some of these tools may appear familiar, as they have been utilized in previous quests and instrumentations of human endeavors towards spiritual fulfillment. The Earth record contains centuries of these higher pursuits, including many ancient and indigenous practices replete with Ascension tools and traditions. After all, humans have, within their soul imprint, the aspirations for the sovereign pursuit of higher consciousness and Source-Revelation. Other tools will be much less familiar and more esoteric, calling to the higher self to engage and prosper. As Cosmic Light showers the planet, additional methods of 5D journeying become increasingly available yet may seem less familiar and more mysterious. Many blueprints have been given by the extraterrestrials who have come to assist Earth in this journey.

Numerous off-planet species have experienced this Ascension process and are living in 5D realities.

As you will discover, the ability to be of service in the 5D is paramount to harmony, happiness, joy and love; therefore, the guides and methods are given with the highest hope of transformation for the human race. Once again the Sacred Figure 8 proliferates its golden threads. The intention and sacredness by which one approaches all 5D pursuits is most important, for readying oneself in sacred aspiration is the gateway for entrance into the domain of the Fifth Dimension experience.

1. MANTRA FOR REMEMBRANCE

Strum the sacred strings within by sounding the High-Heart voice…consecrating inner chambers and permeating the outer void with the vibrational field of 5D reverence. Upon each day's awakening and before each night's slumber, repeat this Mantra to sanctify your own Magnificence, the Ascension Journey and the Oneness of All. Know the language of the Cosmic Light! Remember, with each breath of sacred sound, you seed the Earth with the Light of Divine Presence.

Mantra:
Ohmni Mah: The All of Me
Ohmni Zah: The All of You in Community
Ohmni Rah: The All of Everything
Ohmni Ahhhh: The All of Blissful Pause

2. THE ACCELERATED FUEL OF EARTH'S BOUNTIES

All material of nature abounds with Source Light…interwoven through channels or cosmic-ribbons with the "living imprints" of that material form. Every stone, tree, plant, animal and mineral has unobstructed gateways connecting to "holy-highways" streaming from their living being from beyond. It is only humans living on Earth who have lost the network of sanctified avenues to their living Light Matrix.

Without the "illuminated-messengers" from beyond, is it no wonder that darkness has been able to permeate the field of human endeavors?

The alive beingness of the rock, tree or water comes through into the material world, manifesting its living matrix in the phenomenon of corporeal reality. The matrix of these living beings birth material reality from beyond the quantum level, thus bringing the light of Source creation. The consciousness of these living beings eventually becomes the crystal, plant, water, fire and even air. When humans communicate and bond with nature's bounty, they are convening with conscious beings from the far reaches of cosmic, multidimensional realms. This inspires the vibratory journey to the long lost channels of the human Soul Matrix. As nature's aliveness is felt, a vibrational resonating field is triggered that shimmers, shakes and dissolves locked gates of human consciousness, opening the channels from the living Soul Matrix. In this way, nature "reminds" humans from whence they came! Treat sacred nature's material, and it will lend you the wings of its consciousness to fly into the mysteries of long-forgotten corridors of Life Force energy.

The ties to Source have never been broken within the natural world of Earth and so, as time is spent in these gardens of native wonders, Source connection is realigned, remembered and recharged. This is one of your greatest Ascension tools, as the light-life emanating from Earth is truly sacred beyond time and space. As you open to Earth's bounty, the fuel and recharge comes from the living, breathing dimensions of all material form, translating truths from Universal Source wisdom. This, my friends, will not only save the human race but also reset the beauty and magnitude of the Ascension journey on Earth. The Unity breath of life is fully and deeply experienced in the holy sanctity of your natural world; therefore, we ask, "Can the human race bow in reverence to the very thing they have almost destroyed?"

As stated many times in this book, Earth's bountiful nature provides tremendous balance and wellbeing for humans and all living inhabitants. You might be surprised to know that some extraterrestrials visit Earth just to feel this bounty as their own planets have faded in live vibrancy. Even though the abundance of nature's resources has also diminished on this planet, there is still such beautiful vibrant life that is intricately connected to Source. Now that Earth herself is stepping into the Fifth Dimension, that vibrancy will only accelerate, providing healing and invigorating all that has been lost. Rest reassured that Earth continues her journey with the greater cosmic neighborhood regardless of what humans do, but the beauty and wonder as humans join her and the greater galactic environs will be felt in the far reaches of the Universe. And so, connecting and being in deep conscious relationship with Earth is most crucial at this time…for she whispers of Oneness in her rhythms, sounds, colors and sacred designs.

Ode to Earth—From the Star Beings Above

Oh, Beauteous Earth…how we bow to your most wondrous journey.

Your bold greens and blues…and lustrous hues of life and living breath.

So diverse you are…sprouting life from the riches of your grounded soils.

You shine bright to so many in the Cosmos, yet seen by few who call Earth their home.

Many across the cosmic expanse have come to see you, touch you and simply feel you.

Ah, to see your spinning, swirling, colored sphere from the recesses of space just once, is to know the Divine Presence of Source.

So amazing and wondrous to feel your graceful migration through space, all the while your inhabitants feel total stillness in the space odyssey of planetary motion.

Oh, Beautiful Celestial Being called Earth…you who possesses the most sacred feminine fire to birth life, even in the midst of your own belly burning and shaking.

You have withstood so much and yet have never given up on those that feed upon you.

You provide a womb for birthing the richness of diverse, animated life-forms…staying true to Source mission even when your peoples cannot see you, hear you or bear witness to your incredible lands of fueled, illuminated life force.

Know you have helped raise shimmering hope and faith for many of your planetary brethren in the far reaches of this Universe.

You are the creator, holder and healer of so much new life essence, sprouting the most infinitesimal and grandest imprints for material form to manifest and seed the Universe.

Your steadfastness to remain vital and generative is a blueprint transported to many galaxies beyond so that other celestial planetary beings can once again rise up with the sustenance generated from your very Beingness.

Our gratitude overflows the riverbanks of Cosmic Heart swells.

Know we are here to bear witness to you, to build the Sacred Figure 8 of Magnificent Reflection so that we may nurture you with the magnitude of our Cosmic Love. ♡

3. CRYSTALS AND ESSENTIAL OILS

Crystals

Numerous codes within Earth's crystals and stones have been opened and are alive with the higher energies of Ascension. Their channels to the living soul imprint from whence they came are pulsing with the aliveness of Source connection. While the crystals and stones of planet Earth have never been disconnected from their Source Matrix, they are more enlivened now than ever before due to the immense Diamond Light coming into the planet. You might say, they are on fire with the dancing light of Ascension in action. Work with them, talk with them, hold them and surround yourself with them. Allow them to spark your higher essences and cosmic codes, revealing ancient remembrances of who you are and from whence you came.

Each crystal offers a geometricized design of felt vibrations, stimulating and harmonizing your entire being with healing and regenerative infusions. Experiencing a crystal requires the utilization of your higher *Soul Sensory Modalities (SSM)*. Think of it this way… before entering the communal space for meeting these beings, bring a reverent and sacred field and call upon your higher *SSM* to come into fruited action. Meet the crystal being with this sanctified awareness and feel the vibrant highways of communication begin to open. So you see once again, with those that are Source-aware (in this case the crystal beings), there is a spiraling effect where the more-of-the-crystal manifests the more-of-you!

Some of the crystals on Earth are particular to your planet, creating great curiosity among cosmic travelers regarding these special stones. Some crystals are record-keepers, creating a planetary repository for the true history of Earth. Crystal seers, both on and off planet, can access these most informative and enlightening crystalline libraries…producing roadmaps for the future of Earth. Certain crystals on Earth can also be found elsewhere in the galactic grounds of space and some have been placed on Earth by extraterrestrials for this time now! Many are directly connected with our beautiful star crafts that are currently in the Light Circle surrounding your planet. In particular, lapis lazuli, rutilated quartz and the purple/green fluorites have special connections to our craft; others have direct links to the celestials and angelic presences.

Simply obtaining the meaning of each crystal from books, while informing and directional, is not the same as luxuriating in the crystal's fruited frequencies. You arrived with a crystal/stone reference guide hidden within. Discover this guide once again and dance the magic of the crystalline beings. They are calling to you…listen carefully and follow the trails of the lighted ribbons wafting through your inner chambers. The crystals already have communication with each other even in the farthest regions of space. Their energy is connected through wormholes or channels of the most unimaginable design. In the course of time, you will be able to travel through these channels created by the sovereignty of the crystal dynasty. Carry them with you and you will always have a beacon to space and all her inhabitants. *Ah, the scintillating motion of whirling heightened consciousness created when humans join the crystal inhabitants and together create a sparkling revelation and revolution on Earth.* ♡

Essential Oils

Essential oils are formulated from the beautiful sovereign province of plants. These oils capture the very core essence of a particular plant, thus making available the direct experience through the effusion of the plant's sacred design. Plant essences capture both the living physical and energetic matrixes of these beautiful beings. Think of essential oils as natural healers, soothers and alchemists.

The profusion of nature's bounties coming into being now is infused with extraordinary 5D energies. Plants are amazing heritors of these higher frequency templates and, as such, the essential potions as well. Remember, plants, including trees, are in total alignment with the advanced living matrixes from which they came. They are continually receiving directive energies from that which made manifest their physical form; thus, they are soul connected and have deep remembrances of Source infusion. The plant beings are alive with star illumination as they have a conscious relationship to the cosmic skies above and the astronomical movement of Earth. Plants have a direct knowing of the Sun and the Moon, as you see them lean towards the light, rest in the dark and bend with the winds of motion on the planet. Their essences are full of this heightened consciousness of all that surrounds them!

I will tell you this...there is much yet to be discovered from the magical world of plants. Each plant essence has a particular healing and rejuvenating quality, as has been foretold by many of your indigenous cultures who have known that the sacred materials of earthen origin can heal her inhabitants even when there is not reciprocity. There are many on Earth who have walked the beaded forests and flowered deserts and know the truth of the sacred plants. Follow their path and let your breath become the channel for these gifted aromas as you merge with the beauty of these planted beings that grow upon the bosom of your Earth planet. You might even become the purveyor of unknown landscapes of planted life on your planet.

Plant essences speak in frequency language and grant the opportunity for you to open forgotten receptor sites and create vibrational fields resonating with these beauteous aromas and tinctures. You see, this is yet another moment to partake in the swirling movement of the Sacred Figure 8 with the natural planted beings of Earth. Try out the essential oil of the orange, for it is one of the first fruits to be infused with 5D frequencies. The orange can be an aid in both protective and expansive endeavors. And, of course, the pine plant family, generating essential oils like frankincense, are particularly important now because of the illuminated intensity of the diamond light entering the planet. It is crucial, therefore, to have your third eye and pineal gland open, clear and ready!

Most importantly, take your *Soul Sensory Modalities* on a luscious, sensual journey with plant essences and bathe yourself in the alchemy directly created from *As Above, So Below!* It is beautiful to behold these essences that create evolving aroma, balms, potions, extracts and medicines. Essential oils can create the aromatic fuel for you to resonate with Source connection, cosmic flow and 5D evolution. You have these same connections and matrixes within you. Feel not only the plant but also the oneness of the plant with Mother Earth, her surroundings and the cosmic sphere of life. Certain plants were brought here by ETs to help the planetary being of Earth herself, while others are indigenous to Earth for her inhabitants. How wonderful to simply experience these essences, thus opening your *Soul Sensory Modalities* for traveling the cultivated highways kept clear and open by the sprouted richness of the plants themselves. Breathe in their melodious aromas and enjoy the moment of merger with that which lives in nature. Feel the similar fabric of life stimulated and alive within you, while remembering the plants are beings of immense beauty. Realize that there are Plant Beings from other civilizations in your Universe that are the sentient and the highest intelligent ones on their planets. As you utilize the essential oils of your plant world, know that you are readying yourself for a grand meeting! Imagine a gathering of these Beings made manifest as intelligent Cosmic Beings walking and communicating with many others in the far reaches of the Cosmos. Enjoy!

4. COMMUNITY AS THE HUMAN ACCELERATOR

The cornerstone revelation of a civilization's evolvement is how the "intelligent self-aware" species interacts and treats the inhabitants on their planet. The clearest illustration of a maturing species is found in the very gathering places of their communal endeavors. When humans congregate, it becomes a living laboratory demonstrating the highest and lowest vibrational fields of the heart. The dark/light quotient of a planet can be determined by how humans (in this case) treat one another. It is easy to speculate that Earth has not even reached the halfway mark…illustrating the breeding ground for derisive actions and conditional constraints for many humans. While it is true that humans have demonstrated the most extraordinary love potentialities coming to fruition when in crisis situations and survival-themed circumstances, communal settings occupied with the presence of other humans can be a tricky landscape to navigate. Ancient, historical and familial triggers can instantly be ignited. Old paradigms of deprivation, fear and separation can quickly be inflamed and become the forefront of the neuro-dynamics of the bio-suit fear-template. Lack of trust and safety, with blind detachment for the highest good of all, seem to mark the territory of many community experiences. Transformation of consciousness and High-Heart pursuits must come through to enliven a neoteric sense of Cosmic and Unity principles for communal living. The New Paradigm of Consciousness requires an avant-garde architectural design of visionary thinking, feeling and behaving for the community of humans to move into the cosmic neighborhood of conscious cooperation and inspiration.

The New Paradigm for Communal Togetherness.

Establishing new communities based on High-Heart frequencies of the Fifth Dimension are paramount for establishing the realities of the emerging New Dawn.[1] As humans are able to experience beneficial and light-boosting environments of ascending communities, the readiness-quotient for this consciousness journey will be seen, sown and stirred. Communities are the new fabric by which consciousness transformation can be held and propagated. They provide a new kind of healing and realigning with High-Heart soul principles. *The frequencies felt in 5D community experiences stir and awaken embers of remembrance, igniting candescent fires deep within. The agenda for the New Dawn of Consciousness becomes manifest as the communal experience creates a new reality of being and living.*

In third dimensional realities, however, it is often societal group structures that have caused consequential damage to the Soul and its awakening journey on Earth. There is also much awareness on Earth that the social/emotional architecture created in families, education, religion and business need major revision. Nevertheless, the desire for visionary-revision must further address those potentially sacred gatherings that focus on mental, physical, emotional and spiritual health and wellness. Any time or space occupied with two or more humans can inspire dynamics and dramas that have a rippling effect far beyond those who are physically gathered. This need not be shamed or judged, rather utilized to provide an understanding of

---

[1]The Sanctuary for Evolutionary Vision is one such Sacred 5D Community. For further reference go to: www.theshift.rocks

how communities are incredibly powerful in creating lasting, echoing frequencies within the human experience. Remember, the rumbling vibrations of the human community are felt outside the limits of the space of Earth.

Humans together are quite capable of transforming the terrain upon which they walk and talk. The effects are often robust, enduring and puissant. The question becomes how to utilize your most instrumental tool of Community so that you might weave lasting and vibrant fabrics of love and unity. Know it will be the revamping of these socially designed systems that will offer sacred, reparative experiences to establish the new circuitry of the 5D High-Heart... inspiring all intentions, actions, thoughts and feelings.

There is no question that humans have the capacity to lead with "No Harm and the Highest Good for All." Imagine for a moment feeling the warmth, safety and peace of true, heart-soul comradeship, thus enlivening the highest regard for the growth and wellness for every member of the human community. After all, unity and the miracle of the diversity on the planet give proof to Source inspiration and divination. The 5D community is a reparative, healing and reformative experience, creating anew the template of human evolution and the fertile field for transformation at an eclipsed rate of speed.

Guidelines for the Community Heart necessarily include the manifestation of certain principles of action upon entrance to the community...bringing the following frequencies, notions and potions:

+ No harm and the Highest Good for One and All.
+ Love made visible through Compassion.
+ Openness creating the flow of curiosity and diversity.
+ Joining forces to create the greater-than-one formula for exponential travels.
+ A desire to journey into unknown, mysterious and magical dimensions.

✦ Wonderment for the communal dance…weaving the fabric of the new dimensionality of the Communal Being.

✦ High regard, acceptance and inquisitiveness for Other.

✦ Illuminated Desire for the experience of the Sacred Figure 8 among the human species.

✦ The Magnificence of You.

✦ The act of reflection and receiving the Magnificence of others.

✦ The willingness to be awe-inspired and astonished by your fellow human beings!

As the sacred goals of Unity, Love and Harmony are shared, imagine being among humans with absolute certainty that there is nothing to fear, nothing to hide, nothing to hold back. It feels so miraculous, magical and heavenly that very few would dream of lowering the communal frequency. Therefore, nothing is done, felt or thought that would diminish such buoyancy and lightness of being. When first entering and experiencing these sacred communities, it is very important to curtail, attenuate and abandon old paradigms of diminishment and the ego-matrix. One ego-directed human is capable of lowering the vibration of the group, and who would want to be that one? As each human enters the communal domain of the glimmering vibrational field of 5D Community, the beautiful light attunement and resonation create a synchronistic field inviting and magnetizing the felt movement towards the High-Heart journey. The reparation process of healing and rejuvenation begins as the portals open for the truth of not only who you are but the entire global community of human beings!

Stabilizing and Support of the One Among Community

Without the fiery propellant of communal love, it is impossible to accelerate the Ascension journey on Earth into the new 5D terrain. First, as you travel into more unknown territory to discover remembrances, soul templates and *Soul Sensory Modalities (SSM)*, it will be crucial to have validation and resonation. It is too easy to doubt and stew when left alone, leaving these amazing discoveries as wisps of dreamlike material. When there is less perceived safety, less definition and less familiarity, it is easy to be pulled back into the recognizable 3D world. Knowing there are sojourners with heightened awareness of this most wondrous yet unexplored path is extremely comforting and inspiring. Others offer a reference point that often cannot be found within.

Communities serve as a resonating tuning fork bringing the energy to higher levels of High-Heart majesty. The vibrational fields created by these communal gatherings "turn up the dials" of "realized awareness" for all those present. Scientists are increasingly curious about the power of group gatherings, such as meditations and musical concerts, and their effect on the surrounding morphogenic consciousness field. This is just the tip of the iceberg as you will see and soon experience. Sitting with others who are especially gifted with the *Soul Sensory Modality* of telepathic awareness potentiates that same channel within another. *Soul Sensory Modalities,* DNA code activations and the lighted material of the higher 5D self turn on and tune in. Soul activations are bountiful in the sacred architecture of the High-Heart Community. Many sacred spirals begin to spin between and among community members, inspiring remembrances of incarnations and parallel lives. As humans experience the roller-coaster ride of the Ascension process, it is incredibly beneficial and restorative to feel the spirit and the holding power of community. As frequent dives into the denser, more difficult interludes of 3D interference are inevitable, the steadiness and sure-focused aim of the Communal Template is crucial. Community becomes the revered accelerant to exponentiate the Ascension journey on Earth.

The template created by sacred communal experiences becomes a beacon and magnet of high love and light, steadily bringing each person to a continuous rhythmic heartbeat, striving towards their highest manifestation of all that lies within. This soft but strong embrace of individual magnificence in community is a kiss of heavenly delight. As one allows the sweet, melodious sounds of communal purring to penetrate the bio-suit, it transforms from one of fear to love. Can you envision gatherings no longer filled with the anticipation of negative and toxic invasion, but rather lifting up and moving towards such amazing Harmony and Unity? For one moment, imagine a school where the community of educators offers a liquid growth potion to all students. Teachers gently humming with each breath the truth of the student's brilliance and sanctified-sovereign place and mission in the Universe of living beings. Classrooms creating and reverberating fifth dimensional energy! Vision a spiritual temple of intermutuality and reciprocity where the fabric upon entrance is filled with acceptance, love and unity. This sacred temple is not so much a place but an experience where all humans are seen as Source light. What upliftment could be felt, inspirations experienced and soul essences enlivened! Can you imagine a community of governing legislators meeting to design the sacred exchange for the highest potentialities of its entire people? By the way, on many 5D planets politicians are called Unity technicians. Now vision this: a young student attends High-Heart educational institutions, experiences Source alignment in the temples of sacred alignment and chooses, then, to become a Unity technician for the good of all! Do you think Earth would dance and celebrate such a vision made manifest? This is in Earth's timeline Now. Be this, and you shall see this! Eventually you will create a Community of Unity that will then be within the blossoming bosom of the One. ♡

Ushering in Global Consciousness.

As communities become the new fabric of 5D experience, this produces a "lightening" rod for global peace and unity. These communities begin to create morphogenic fields of the most intense magnitude...ushering in *global* transformation of consciousness on Earth. The global network then serves as a tuning fork for all who live upon the Earth, creating a new symphony of voices...resounding in every corner, habitat and circle of living beings. This will be a cosmic milestone, an illuminated metamorphic event, where all interactions of inhabitants on Earth will be silhouetted with glimmering soul glow. The unique frequencies of the New Paradigm of community living become the life sustenance and fertile ground by which everything can grow. The ultimate spirally dance of *one* nourishing *all* and the *all* nourishing *one* makes Life Force indistinguishable as it lives everywhere and in everything. Individuals raising community consciousness… communities raising global consciousness and, finally, planetary Unity creating transcendence into the New Cosmic Dawn.

The Sanctity of Source Awareness

Without the experience of other in total buoyant flight, it is very difficult to move past the dense, gravitational pull of 3D self-entrenchment. Community offers a splendid and most sublime opportunity for the whirling movement of spirited-intimacy in the Sacred Figure 8 of 5D frequencies. How heavenly to feel no fear, no diminishment, no hesitation, but instead to fly in the highest energetic fabric of you with another. Can you stay seated in your most magnificent self as you merge with that same magnificence in another? *Knowing and feeling the glimmering beauty of both while still self-aware is such astounding practice for maintaining presence while meeting Divine Source.* Sacred community offers what has not been offered before… becoming a portal for multidimensional travel, all the while cocooned in the presence of others while soaring with the Now presence of soul spirit. After all, you have been infused with illuminated Divinity every time the light of a Heart-Being touched you. *It is a beautiful prospect that experiencing one another in High-Heart frequencies creates a sacred stencil for reuniting Soul with Source!*

From Global to Cosmic Community

The most auspicious and prosperous outcome of the Sacred Human Community on Earth is the expansion into the Galactic

Community Experience. The realization of "others" in the outer bounds of your Universe may be the most important discovery of your planet's inhabitants. To know you are not alone and to become a revered member among many off-planet civilizations is quite a revelation…yes? The sharing of information alone will be monumental and exalting. You will quickly progress into new solutions of wonder and awe, moving past what has ailed Earth (disease, global warming, hunger, injustice and war). This will indeed shed light on Earth's new timeline expeditiously coming into being. It will be a revelation that will lead to enormous amounts of information about your cosmic surroundings and, in this new understanding of star-sphere wisdom, you will begin to treat Earth with more reverence and wonder. Diversity will become celebrated, revered and embraced. Curiosity will lead your thoughts and actions. Standing in openness will become the warrior stance. Growth and expansion will be in the very heart of the human fabric. Love and Light will become the resonating frequencies tendered. So you see, when you learn to laugh, play and be together as a human race, you have much to look forward to! *This new cosmic operatic performance will be playing in the theaters beyond space and time and will be interactive, participatory and heart-lifting. Spirit will be the common energetic bond, love will be the offering at every turn and the applause will be heard in the beat of the Universal Heart.* ♡

5. TIME/SPACE RATIOS

Humans spend an inordinate amount of time/space in third dimensional pursuits that continue to provide opaque veils, obfuscating the soul-path and decreasing visible motion. Activities in the 3D time/space domain solidify and ground you in the denser planes of reality. Aspiring to higher frequency pursuits dissolves the web of imprisoned consciousness and enhances the ability to move into new time/space coordinates. These etheric and buoyant junctures allow the effervescent Now to catapult into fifth dimensional creative movement. Of course there are many 3D pursuits that are joyous and delicious, and these often create jumping-off points for experiencing higher vibrational fields. However, you must be quite a subtle detective to know when you are jumping into the oblivion of comatose consciousness versus striving towards increasing the fertile gardens of spiritual blooming.

This is the time of the New Dawn and, therefore, a careful assessment of time/space ratios is most crucial. If you only observed one day of time/space in your life, would the compass reveal elevated directions of higher, lower or "maintenance" vibrational states? The object is to increase the ratio towards those people, events, activities and surroundings that multiply higher frequencies within one's inner state. How much time and space do you dedicate to 3D maintenance versus 5D enhancement? Perhaps it's time to reassess just how you take up time and fill up space. See time as your fellow passenger, bending into it to see the winds of change. Go with it, not against it. Understanding the infinite nature of your consciousness will help you know you have all the time in the world or, for that matter, the Universe. Be in time and follow the moment of Now. The Now moment is imbued in the fabric of the Universal voyage beyond the crossing point of time/space consciousness. Care to take a ride in the space of *realized awareness?*

Cues and Rituals

Cues: Enhance your living space so it reflects your higher consciousness. As most homes are designed to call you outward, let your surroundings emit a radiance that calls you inward. Change your environment so you can see yourself and your higher synchronic soul path in all that envelops you. You will be amazed how this bolsters and supports the Ascension journey, leaving you more time to be in the fertile field of expanded consciousness.

Rituals: Create daily rituals that remind you that you are indeed on a revolutionary adventure. Be aware of routines that root you more solidly in denser emotions or thoughts. Invent new habits and practices that inspire the High-Heart to sing in the refined octaves of the Sublime. Begin to tip the scales of your time quotas to build the golden ratio of time/space and the frequency essence of your Ascension adventure will pour forth. In this way, you pave the path to No-Time of the Now.

Bio-Suit

It is most crucial to observe time spent in your bio-fear suit versus time spent building your bio-love suit. The bio-fear suit is the most common body, mind, heart framework. This suit has been wired to respond to fear, fright and survival. As consciousness evolves, the bio-suit of a species begins to transform, creating inner networks that lean towards the lighted way of love. You might think it is your nature to "freeze, fight or flight" but your soul would dictate another path. Pausing in life from the stimuli that solidifies the bio-fear template is crucial, as you can't build anew while still drenched in the automated pathways of antiquated responding. The fear bio-suit response system is often right below conscious awareness and, therefore, becoming cognizant of that which triggers this old mechanism is crucial. Changing the biological templates within affects the mind and heart, innervating and spurring spirit to charge the body with new circuitry of the bio-love template. This, in turn, makes the body lighter, mind clearer and the heart brighter.

Changing the Structure of the Bio-Suit

+ *Movement* carries the winds of change and transformation. Make sure to experience movement through space every day. Whether driving, walking, running or dancing, let movement bring new life to the body, traversing the past stuck, stubborn and entrenched neuro-networks of the material world. The migratory flow of dynamic locomotion also brings remembrances of other incarnate lives that are roaming with you through space and time. Ignite the inner imprints of flying and crafting through time/space!

✦ *Stillness* in space creates the potentiality of enlivening the movement of consciousness.

✦ *Pausing* in time allows the connective material for consciousness travel. Take a moment for deep breathing, feeling the in-breath of All That Is and the out-breath of All That Is You. Let this Unity Breath pause all systems for re-timing and re-spacing.

✦ *Yoga and its related movement of sacred postures* stretch the body beyond its current condition, bringing life, invigoration and innervation to the inner body landscape and adding new passageways to Now presence. Each posture creates a vibrational field that not only releases debris and dross, but also forms the new terrain in the material fabric of your physical form. Yoga inspires the material body to expand its neuro-circuitry into the new bio-suit of love, peace and serenity.

✦ *Massage and Bodywork* to sculpt and heal the body engenders full attention to the new bio-suit of rest, safety, calm and the gentle embrace of compassion. Allowing another to facilitate moments of complete surrender, while maintaining one's sovereignty, resets bodily *light-fluids*.

✦ *Sound* generates and holds frequencies of the sacred designs of universal flow. Let nature's songs and the music of the planet carry you to sweet lullabies of love, quenching the thirst for ancient echoes of All That Is. Listen carefully to harmonious sound vibrations coming from beyond your dimensional space and time. A whispered message on the wings of wind, music without a player, ringing or buzzing visiting the inner pathways of the ear or soft voices when no one is there are manifestations of visitors from afar. These are but a few of the touching notes outside the limits of your current reality, transfiguring the ability to travel to a new time and a new space.

These soul-designing methods, and there are many more, change the inner landscape of your bio-suit, moving from fear to love and solidity to fluidity. Begin your travels on mysterious expeditions to find new treasures of transforming the integrity and sanctity of the human material body. Allow one month to practice these time/space exercises without goals, without destinations, without ideas about where you will land. And remember, if you are doing something for the distinction or destination, you will only experience the ghost-energy of the Now... half-spent, half-present, half-felt. Let go of time and begin to learn how to travel in the Now atmosphere. You can't change time/space ratios without this ultimate paradox: *the time of no space and the space of no time!* Be this and plan on being delighted, joyous and ever so close to seeing that which is **beyond** your time and space!

6. TRAVELING IN THE UNKNOWN

Traveling in the Unknown is a most interesting, yet crucial, tool conducive to navigating and creating the very fabric for 5D realities. There is much bewilderment and mystery still surrounding the Fifth Dimension and so becoming comfortable and adept with unrecognized, unperceived and "alien" phenomena is quite imperative for crossing into 5D realities.

The 3D is full of contradictory and paradoxical paradigms of thinking and this is made apparent in the province of mystical journeying. On the one hand, it seems difficult to encounter unknown, strange or odd phenomena without being suspect and apprehensive. This creates a huge trigger for fleeing to the comforts and familiarity of the 3D world...a world where so much is understood, albeit limited and defined by something that has now passed. Receding into familiar habits and patterns when faced with mystifying and incomprehensible information thereby becomes a place of felt safety and security. Yet on the other hand, humans have shown much tenacity and great courage for moving into uncharted and undiscovered territory. The explorer archetype has shown up in many scientific, artistic and healing endeavors, catapulting humans to new lands on Earth and now in space. How beautiful to have such beings among you. Yet, adapting to new ways of thinking and feeling takes great effort and fortitude. *Perhaps knowing that the very survival of planet Earth depends on solutions found in fifth dimensional realities will help galvanize and spark the determination and fearlessness required for these mysterious, foreign and exotic travels.*

Designing and engaging in activities that are less known and less familiar are important steps for entering this sacred uncharted land. Drive on unfamiliar roads, see new sights, hear new sounds, learn something you have never known before. At least once a day, explore something mysterious, strange, puzzling or alchemistic, and feel the rising states of being that ensue. As you do this, the tethers of the 3D world will slowly detach allowing a buoyant, floating experience provided by the new surveillance of this *unknown* vibrational field. It is amazing how familiar terrain can cause sleepy, anesthetized awareness or trigger land mines of remembrances of things long gone. The path less trodden will create acute perceptions of the Now reality. Do not be afraid to get lost in order to be found in the inner workings of mysterious voyaging. Surviving and thriving in the *unknown* is the destination and the journey all at once.

Remember, simply being in the *unknown* template is a frequency experience. Becoming familiar with this *"unknown-frequency"* is key to readying oneself for the inexplicable, mystifying 5D vibrational field. Developing comfort with this awe-inspiring, enigmatic state is one of the most important tools for Ascension! Embracing strange, esoteric, foreign and even bizarre phenomena creates an inner template that eventually becomes both familiar and expansive. What a beautiful paradox happening all at once! The practice of "unknown-journeying" increases one's comfort and curiosity, eventually establishing a place of peace and openness to the 5D experience. You will have the elasticity of movement in your very being that will enable you to hold the invisible, mystical world of the New Dawn. As you become familiar with strange lands of being, thinking and feeling, the invisible world will take shape and form. The great unease and fear often generated in the 3D when presented with such material will dissipate, enabling one to move further into the mysterious rather than backtracking into that which is known and familiar. *As the unknown becomes more intriguing and enticing, free will of the Sovereign Self can reach into the vast landscape of universal resources to create new realities of manifested resonating fields coming into being. You are the landscaper in these mystifying gardens of the New World!*

The very experience of *unknown-frequencies* not only creates building blocks for the new realities, it also forges channels or corridors towards gateways of the Fifth Dimension. Think of these as unknown roadways towards that which soon will be known. You can see that traveling these corridors with a steady yet determined pace is most essential for entrance to the New Age of Consciousness. As you experience peace and a strange familiarity of the weird and freaky worlds beyond the known, the future will come tumbling down the path, greeting you with unexpected resiliency and joy. The two sides of the coin, the unknown and known, soon become the whole of All that is…neither displaying two sides nor one but instead creating an alternate third reality where the *unknown-frequency* becomes the known path towards unraveling and revealing mysteries that are never-ending and ever more apparent.

And so, *unknown-frequencies* become associated with accelerated growth and expansion, quickly becoming a desirable state of being. You may find yourself spending enormous amounts of time in the spontaneous, unplanned, unexpected, impromptu moments of life all leading to the entrance of an immense, magical, pleasurable and surprising world. Allowing your inner field to take up more and more space and time rather than the externalized known space and time taking up you, you become less encumbered and freer! Instead of being driven by externalized signs and directions, the All of You creates the maps and becomes the driver of this star-pointed voyage. Now, it might be tempting to return to the 3D to search for something you have lost or left behind. Most likely you will only discover that you spent much labor letting go and detaching from these known quantities so you could indeed be free and gain the buoyancy necessary to lift into the 5D, forever altering the quality of life. Remember, the 3D is where your ego lives, ruling and spending much time searching for something it doesn't have. On the other hand, the soul lives and governs with gentleness and fierceness in the 5D...searching for nothing for all has been discovered within. *So, the path of the unknown reveals the known of the multidimensional, ever-expansive world.*

Imagination: The Vehicle for Illuminated Travel

Imagination makes visible that which has been invisible and is sparked by the seed of consciousness. It is an elucidating, illuminating vehicle in which to travel towards these inner highways of higher dimensional realities. Allowing the felt experience of consciousness wafting through the hallways of imagination and waking-dream frequencies opens unknown territories. It is important to note that you can't imagine anything that does not already exist in the realm of the higher consciousness; however, once in complete 5D consciousness, you do become the creator of *new* realities spanning across time/ space constraints, birthing some new image from the All of You. So, *imagination creates images of that which exists just beyond what is already known.* How extraordinary! Therefore, have plenty of fuel and time for elongated imaginary experiences, for they will bring you to the new lands of the New World. Make sure there are no intrusive passengers sneaking a ride from your thought domain, as they will only diminish and subvert your new, light-filled dreams of magic yet to come.

The human body, heart and brain are of incarnate, finite material, whereas consciousness is infinite. The gate or portal opening to this expanded consciousness sits in the pineal gland with outgoing visionary flow through the third eye. Here is a brief exercise to brighten your imaginative powers: *Sit quietly and begin to connect with the pineal gland in the center of your brain/mind field. Allow it to open and feel the fluidity of the crystalized light energy begin to sparkle and glimmer. Imagine a portal forming, opening a channel directly to your third eye chakra. Then, see this white, spiraling, illuminated tunnel moving up and out. Become part of it and observe the Cosmos unfolding with brilliant stars. As you revel in this most wondrous experience, see a vast horizon coming towards you. Migrate towards this lighted crossing point where the mystical, invisible realm begins. Here consciousness is the only phenomenon and joy the felt experience. You simply ARE…entering the invisible realms of multidimensional potentialities. Take the roof off the vehicle of imagination now and feel the wind move through your very being. What visions come? What experiences are felt? Imagine other worlds and feel the truth of your expansiveness. Now…bring this back to Earth and know you have paved the roads for Ascension on Earth.*

7. TRANSPARENCY AS A TOOL

Transparency releases and frees the soul for the soaring flight towards total visibility. You are here on Earth to act from such a freed soul! The ability to become transparent is an astounding tool that unveils and liberates the magnificent higher self. The Universe is in total transparency, yet it is quite amazing that it still can't be seen in Totality because the veils have not been lifted in the eyes of the beholders. It is inspiring to note that as transparency becomes the path, the Universe becomes more seen, heard and experienced in all its beauty. Spiraling transparency with another, whether a human, planet or the cosmos, causes *the one* to be seen and this ability to be seen opens the channel whereby *the other* can be seen as well.

When you live through crystalline presence, the heavy veils of 3D living simply dissolve, opening gates to reveal and be the translucent light being that you are. There is nothing to hide. The energy it takes to cloak, mask and suppress your inner being is simply enormous. Shielding is such a common experience that it becomes part of the very fabric of identification. In the 3D, it feels safe and sheltering to live behind the shield, and protection becomes more familiar than Unity. You can't have Unity without transparency! It is such a paradox that the nontransparent shielding is produced to protect you from rejection, exclusion and judgment and yet the very *field of the shield* keeps you separated and alone. Unification and freedom of flight arrives when there is nothing to hide, nothing to shame, nothing to judge. This, my friends, IS the Fifth Dimension. All at once, you can breathe effortlessly and abundantly, finally connecting to the All of One. Remember, the results of concealed shielding produce far more suffering than the imagined fears of being seen.

Utilize this tool of Transparency and accelerate your path towards the New Human of the Fifth Dimension. Begin with self-transparency in the following ways:

+ Can I recognize when I am shielding? There is a definite felt frequency when you are living in the sheltered and concealed chamber. It is so familiar that you may think it is simply part of your makeup and your place of residence. Pause often, relax your shoulders, breathe deeply and allow a deeper part of you to be known and felt. It matters not whether it is worthy or unworthy, it is yours and yours alone to feel and hold. Whether a knowing, a feeling or a missing or wanting, be with it and do not shield it from your own consciousness. Know that under each layer, you will discover something so relieving and enlightening as the guidance and revelations bring illuminated wisdom. Remember, what lies within is not what it seems but everything is a clue! Allow yourself to feel free to be the All of You.

+ Can I become more aware and conscious of that which lives far below the shielding boundaries, so that I might begin to see the hidden beauty and magnificence of soul's presence? Recognize the cue of the shielding frequency and utilize this to mobilize smooth passage through the marooned pieces of hidden parts to find the Whole and the Holy you.

Do you think you could harm another living being or yourself if you felt your soul presence lighting up your inner chambers and guiding you towards compassion, peace and unity? Transparency of self leads to the very heart of who you are, why you are here and what you are here to do. Do not be fooled by outside structures that want to diminish and demand only the silhouette of the shadowed self. You see, transparency is the key to the total flight of spirit.

✦ As I am transparent with myself, can I gather the courage to be that in the world? Vision dancing with total freedom alongside all beings that you meet…nothing bad, shameful or unworthy, and nothing to be hidden in clandestine corners. Recognize that shielding is a form of *soul-genocide*. It dampens Life Force, leaving the rolled-up, diminished self to slowly die. Oh, how many unspent moments of spirited life have been discarded on the empty dance floor of life. Know that as each human takes flight in unbridled pellucidity, a ripple effect begins to build into a soul tsunami, transforming the very face of the Earth.

As transparency becomes the modus operandi of the human race, reverence, sacredness and gentleness for merging and flowing will be more pronounced, curtailing and dwindling 3D dualities and polarized frequencies of separation. Without transparency, it is a cumbersome, delayed and laborious process, condemning the soul for wanting the lightness of being felt in the buoyancy of the lighted moon. The tool of Transparency is indeed one of the most important methods for Unity Consciousness. Use it to ride the slipstreams of the Ascension journey. It will be a deliberate, easeful and shortest path for coming home! ♡

8. SYNCHRONICITY: RIDING THE SLIPSTREAMS OF THE COSMIC WEB

Upon arrival in an incarnation, the greatest tool available is the ability to utilize *realized awareness.* This heightened consciousness holds the potentiality for one to look and see the breadth and depth of the synchronistic Universe. This experience of realizing the truth of the unfolding Cosmic Web that surrounds and envelopes the All of Everything is quite astounding. For in that moment, you are One with it All, creating Unity where there was separation. In that knowing, there is an understanding that everything is forever coupled and divined from Source. Know that the All of this is summoning you even when you cannot hear, touching you even when you cannot feel, imagining you even when you cannot see. You might understand why, then, it is great practice to comprehend the harmonic convergence of so many entangled events and happenings. The Universe has an amazing ability to call us…is there anyone home to answer?

A journal is a helpful tool for documenting this incoming "cosmic-data." Do you see repeating numbers, letters, symbols or particular clock times? Are events strewn with "coincidental" and fortuitous encounters? Do you see connections appearing that were previously hidden? If you have an especially astute, telepathic communication system, track your thoughts or feelings of others and see where they "pop-in." Follow these mysterious clues and they will lead you to important converging moments that serve your life well.

The Universe has an amazing telegraph service. Learning to decipher the sacred encryptions is an invaluable, vital task. Think of it this way: life is a grand scavenger hunt for discovering and unraveling the synchronistic clues to an end game that is only a beginning! As you track these perceived "pop-ins" from the Cosmic Web, you will not only have access to the greater picture of your life and mission but the grander picture of the Universe itself. Remember, *nothing is what it seems, but everything is a clue!* Have fun mapping these repeating patterns, chance encounters and emerging inlays, for they tell a story that has been hidden until now. All of this is evidence of this grand

Web of Universal design and you are part of it. Become a connoisseur of synchronistic appearances and you will find a road map that you created before you arrived!

As 3D veils thin out, there will be more awareness of telegraphic messages and the frequencies they imbue. Before you search for meaning, however, it is crucial at the moment a synchronic "pop-in" occurs to feel the vibrations that ensue. As you experience repeating numbers, letters, connections and events, note what and how your vibrational field shifts. These incoming pieces of data are bringing frequency states from the world beyond. Receiving these frequency "downloads" and consciously registering them is crucial and most enlightening. Allow these vibrational states to carry you to the messaging where you can decipher the significant meaning and potential implication of these sacred encryptions. First, these messages from beyond carry with them a frequency state creating a 5D experience. Second, the substance and symbolization of them bring expansiveness and augmented meaning to your current realities. Finally, you can then recreate these frequency states all on your own, utilizing them to consciously initiate the voyage back to the Cosmic Web.

The more synchronistic events you become aware of, the greater the inner channel or cosmic tube to the Cosmic Web is expanded and widened. One day you will utilize the frequency state itself (of the synchronic experience) to surf the channels of the Cosmic Web. In this way, you can gather firsthand knowledge of the truth from where you came and where you are centered. You will then not have to wait for synchronic pop-ins to be made apparent, as you will be living, and eventually creating, harmonic concurrences in your life and all that surrounds you. The channel by which you are connected to the Synchronistic Cosmic Web will expand, thus forming the Sacred Figure 8 with all that surrounds and is within you. Ah, rebirthing consciousness of always and forever!

SUMMARY

Utilize these Ascension tools with mindfulness, sacredness and reverence. The higher octave of resolute conscious intention catapults these experiences into full reparation and revelation. These tools hold *frequency signatures* that offer *experiences* of ascended vibrational fields. *Frequencies alter experience and the experience alters and creates a new reality.* Within them is a shifting reality spectrum that moves forward towards conscious expansion and High-Heart living, thus creating the material for the dawning of fifth dimensional realities.

This is not a journey with an arrival stamp of a distant time and space. It is a journey to *be* somewhere and the where is the whirling movement of time/space dispersing into the ethers of the ever-present Now. Waiting for arrival is no longer required, for you are the destination via your higher consciousness. Everything in your world carries vibrant higher consciousness fields…music, art, nature, movement, creative inventions and even the communities in which you gather. The eve of discovering new methods, designs and practices is upon you. Explore and unearth your own passageways for igniting the Ascension fires within and utilize them to BE in both the frequencies of their higher domain and the High-Heart of you. It is in the spiraling motion felt within these illuminated frequencies of living-breath that births 5D realities of Ascension. Join and Be-Hold this fuel for expansion, integration and transfiguration. *Everything is frequency in the dance of the Universe!*

Chapter 8

A Picture for Tomorrow

The Unknown Becomes Known, the Mysteries Become Revelations and the New World Becomes You!

The picture of today is simply the night before the New Dawn. The denser energy of yesterday is leaving the Earth plane and, in the foggy mist, there appears to be chaos, crisis and division. These opaque and disguised energy fields are rising up to be seen and dismantled. Do not look with despair upon the confusion, doubt and derisiveness that encircles the Earth, as all must come to the surface where the new light can dissolve, move and transform the situation. Transparency of the dark is as important as transparency of the light. As the human race aspires to the higher ground of dignity, integrity, justice and unity, a restored frequency of peace, wellbeing and love will lead the way. The collisions and destruction currently on the planet are merely part of the arching movement of the new consciousness. *As the old is no longer feasible for sustaining life and breath, the ever-stretching dynamism of higher consciousness moves from illusion to reality.* A great transposition is currently happening on Earth. Know the changing tides are an absolute sign of the fertile days to come.

The global shift is no different from the personal shift. It takes great courage to shed the skin worn during limiting past times. It is even more arduous for transformative global shifting as it comes with great tumult and turbulence and often creates pandemonium. *In a desperate attempt to discover the exactness of external realities, remember to search and see the truth from the soul-light template within, for this is where new realities will be born.* Seek respite from the old ideologies that are breaking apart and, in this deluge of fallen pieces, find solace in the Illuminated Heart. See this as the Great Shift. Know and stay steady with this renewed emergence. Take a deep, aerated breath and allow the light of the New Dawn to birth within you. As you permit and empower the inner template to shift to the sacred blueprints of love and grace, the germinated seed will sprout new growth thus replacing the chaos and debris. Know the current truth of old paradigms is disintegrating and falling into the Earth, thereby fertilizing something new. That which happens in nature is now happening in consciousness!

COSMIC ILLUMINATION STREAMING UPON THE EARTH

Sacred Cosmic Light is streaming from many origins from the heavens above. Downloads of smart light and the transformational diamond light are causing a rapid shift in metamorphic transfiguration on the planet. The human evolution of consciousness taking place now is opening and expanding a myriad of light portals, thus enabling the reception of this immense and accelerated cosmic light. Rest assured, each step of human transformative action is greeted with more Cosmic-Aid. Because the sovereignty and free will of each being is crucial to this process, the consciousness evolution of the human species has always been the determinant of such Cosmic-Aid. You see, you have always been in the driver's seat! Now it becomes a "realized" choice that manifests the direction and journey of your High-Heart opening and your expanding consciousness.

These illuminated, celestial light-streams are accelerating your DNA activations and opening the code-seeds within you that will dissolve the "one-placement" personality and open the soul-flow within. The "one-placement" personality signifies those particular contours and forms that prescribe and describe a person from one incarnate life. You are here to go beyond this particular placement… you might say you have needed to utilize the one-placement to anchor here and now in this time/space configuration. Nevertheless, you are now ready to unfurl your beautiful wings of Ascended Light and blossom into the infinite Soul-Illuminated Self.

Meditate on the incoming slipstreams of the lighted ribbons and let the remembrances spring forth and stretch into the soul-fluid stream throughout your entire being…body, mind, heart and spirit. *At last, the Soul-Illuminated Self and the Universal Cosmic Spiral move in synchronistic swirling motion together, creating the music of the higher spheres.* Let the lighted seeds within sprout forth towards the fifth dimensional state of Being-ness. Feel the heightened frequencies of the light and develop your *Soul Sensory Modalities (SSM)* to come online and begin to see, feel and hear the new fabric of being 5D.

As channels open to the lighted cosmic-waves of the Universe, the mysterious, multidimensional, sacred blueprints will be available and downloaded. Know that the 3D mind cannot comprehend this. Do not look for this transformation within your current constructs for, by definition, they are within the dawning of your 5D self. At this very moment, however, you are developing the advanced circuitry to download and interpret the new information. Can you pause to feel this vibrational shift? It will be a *frequency experience* and this will become the *reality of consciousness. Become a vehicle for this transmission and spawn awareness of the infinite consciousness of you…only in this state is the reception clear.* Allow this to become you and feel your expanded field in the infinite Universe. ♡

The Liberation of Energy

Energy freed from 3D labors will be most potent and available for 5D designing. This unfettered and liberating process will feel like escaping gravity and levitating in Light Being-ness. It may be shocking at first, for the heaviness of the denser planes has simply been part of the fabric of you.

It will be quite mind-blowing to realize this weighted-ness you have carried is not you after all, but simply the gravitational pull of the denser energy domain. *The outline of self will become less contoured by the denser material energies and more shaped by the lighter buoyancy of the spiritual energy carried by the soul.* This realization will take some time and adjustment, so make sure there is pause enough for joy and delight playing in the illuminated field of You. Manifestation principles will not only be truly understood and available for all, but will be in alignment with higher principles of Unity Consciousness. The new reality will begin to take shape:

❖ Sustaining life will be easeful and natural, and so one life can extend into centuries. As this unfolds, Soul Matrix light will infuse this incarnation even more. The lessons of 3D living simply disappear as you adjust to the new lighted-weight domain of the 5D. *More will be known in living this one life and so less will need to be known by living other lives.* Soul Matrix awareness will increase exponentially. By the way, this will be the first step in sixth dimensional Enlightened Awareness.

❖ Cities will be built where the very skyline will please and soothe the inner landscape of the soul. Earth's vistas will feed your soul and be in constant motion with you, and the planet will receive sustenance simply by your presence!

❖ Livelihood and nurturance from energy fields of those around you will sustain and invigorate your life. Solid foods will become less necessary as the etheric energy fields of all things will be ingested and felt more. There will be "sustenance" devices that interact with your consciousness, thereby creating nourishing foods that are perfectly aligned for enlivening the body, mind and heart.

❖ Designs and devices currently found in your material world will provide the directional path upon which consciousness becomes the vehicle for generating all things conceived and built. For example:

• Equipment for moving and lifting will be replaced by the inner *consciousness-equipment* of levitation and telekinesis *(elevated-consciousness)*. Time saved will be time paused to create anew.

- The "inner-eye" of the domain of your *SSM* will see into the farthest reaches of space *(telescopic-consciousness)* and the inner landscapes of the body *(microscopic-consciousness)*. Energy seers will detect energy patterns produced by the body and help unblock or move them to be in total alignment with health and wellbeing. X-ray vision will be a gift by the body technicians of the future. Quantum realms will be understood and mapped through the realized awareness of the 5D circuitry itself *(quantum-consciousness)*.

❖ Art and music will be designed and performed by consciousness itself *(creative-consciousness)*. The brush will paint in synchronistic movement and the instrument will play in symphonic action with consciousness as the conductor, producer and creator. Artistic endeavors will take less time, as the creative process itself becomes the time of the Now. Nevertheless, there will be many creative venues that you will want to continue in order to feel the aligning movement of the physical experience. Ah, to feel consciousness of Now leading the dance, the painting, the music. You can begin to see the power and beauty that soul manifestation beholds!

❖ Cities of light waves and websites of consciousness exchange will be created. Telepathic light grids that regenerate rather than deplete the user will replace phones and all kinds of electronics.

❖ Currently, there are human spaceships traveling as a result of the inventions of propulsion, anti-gravity and zero-point energy. Soon crafts will be built propelled by consciousness alone, thus untethered by buttons, controls or levers of physical design. These crafts (alive with their own consciousness) will travel throughout the Cosmos in crystalline, vibrational wormholes. Interdimensional travel beyond the speed of light will be possible. You will find the speed of consciousness is quite instantaneous *(interdimensional-consciousness)*. How extraordinary to travel to other planetary systems of magnificent life…but, oh, to jump into multidimensional realms is quite another journey!

❖ Time travel *(bilocated consciousness through time)*: Once grounded in the truth and experience of infinite consciousness, you will begin to understand and utilize time travel. After all, time/space is a woven fabric within you and so learning to ride those slipstreams boosts the potentiality for traveling to other times and other places. The fabric of higher consciousness holds these frequency stations that are initially available through dream, imaginative and meditative states. In altered states of consciousness, it is easy to access the time/space continuum in order to discover other incarnations and parallel lives. This time-journeying weaves ribbons of quantum material for developing *realized awareness* of the whole/holy Soul Matrix. It is a beautiful paradox that the gates to time travel are only found in the illuminated moment of Now. Without passing through the glimmering frequency of Now consciousness, it is impossible to move with and through time. As you learn the motion of *migratory consciousness,* the energetic body will travel through time so you actually *experience* "living" in that time. This may feel a bit dizzying and baffling, but holding this with reverence and curiosity is paramount to entering this new *Soul Sensory Modality* of time-traveling consciousness.

❖ Teleportation *(bilocated-consciousness through space)*: As your body becomes lighter, mobile and buoyant, you can soar past the gravitational pull of the 3D and travel interdimensionally to another location or space expanse. Teleportation brings bilocation to a whole new level. Instead of stepping into a dematerializing/rematerializing device, your consciousness will become the compass, guide and fuel for transporting your body to other Earth and cosmic localities. However, as long as you are tethered to time/space constraints "out there" it will be most difficult to break these barriers and utilize your travel vehicle (pure consciousness) to leap into the mystery realm. Consciousness provides the energetic field in which to travel beyond 3D constructs and restrictions. What a beautiful and magical experience to come!

New Field of Energy

The very act of being in the frequency of expanded 5D conscious-ness will create innovative templates of energy that have never before been on Earth. As a civilization goes through the process of becoming united in consciousness, exoteric and newly configured vibrational blueprints are manifested that will skyrocket the metamorphic journey of that species and the planet as a whole. You will no longer sit in the bleachers in passive observation but will create, design, direct and star in this grand Earth play.

This new frequency on the planet will, in and of itself, be healing, resolving and produce alchemic transformation as if overnight. It will bring neoteric illumination to every problem, dilemma and old paradigm. This shift in light consciousness will produce advanced and enlightened resolutions to current problems on Earth. These elucidated, energetic templates will then create and produce the new architecture for the Fifth Dimension. Consciousness will be the new sculptor's hand forming transmuted contours to be seen through the eyes of the *Soul Sensory Modalities* of the New Human. Can you begin to see them on the horizons of your mind? How exciting that the very act of *conscious-will* spawns a rippling wave of untold magnitude that instantaneously resolves and unites old, polarized factions of partially made pathways. Can you begin to imagine a fusion of evolved consciousness itself with High-Heart ignited fuel forming an alchemic, energy signature never before experienced on Earth? This vibrational signature generates and produces all solutions...all antidotes...all elixirs for the healing and regeneration of Earth and her inhabitants. You can see why this cannot be born of 3D thinking and feeling. To have faith in this new energy field is to acknowledge the plan and purpose of Divine Source. Can you allow your *Soul Sensory Modalities* to open, feel and see this new-energy source forming on Earth? Hear its whispers in the voice of splendid love, see the lighted portals in the billowing clouds above, touch the fabric of renewed winds and taste the sweetness of its pristine breath. It is already here...within you. ♡

This new field of energy will create waves of frequencies moving out into the Cosmos, signaling other galactic civilizations that the magnificence of Soul Consciousness is expanding and transforming on Earth and beyond. It will restart, refresh and reenergize other galactic planetary cultures. After all, they have been waiting for you to awaken, just as you have waited for the emergence of others in the Cosmos so that you might receive the galactic light from the *frequency-frontiers* of these illuminated Souls. This incoming streaming of the fifth dimensional birth quickens your journey and eases your entrance into the galactic neighborhood of cosmic sojourners. As these invigorating cosmic templates of new-fashioned energy burst forth on the planet, humans will leap into the *experience* of Unity Consciousness, thus conceiving its *reality* on Earth. The resulting migratory action will open portals to many extraterrestrial civilizations and signal the time of the Great Disclosure!

GALACTIC COMMUNITY

Recognize first, there is a vibrational field surrounding you now that holds communications from the lighted Universe of life. There are calls to you from the galactic beings surrounding you, and every day they come in many forms. As consciousness is expanded and fluid, these calls will be heard and answered. Dreams and imagination are your most available tools and your pineal gland is the door to the infinite living Universe. Open and plan to be surprised.

Numerous civilizations have sent ambassadors to the Earth plane, and many reside in the cosmic Light Circle surrounding your planet. Some are already living on planet Earth and others have retreated to the inner Earth realms to make calibrated changes to support and bolster your planet's journey into the higher consciousness of the Fifth Dimension. Know that the ETs are in perfect synchronicity with Earth's energetic template. And, many ETs have already established connections and communication corridors with living beings on Earth.

There are amazing ETs who are here to have beautiful relationships with the Elemental realm on Earth. Earth fairies, for example, have been in communion with the ET Elfin culture for quite some time and are returning to their rightful place on the planet. They are extremely responsive to telepathy, as well as physical gestures that demonstrate a desire to communicate with them.

Insectoid beings, like the mantis and vibratory sound insect beings, are working with many of the anthropoid species, such as bees, butterflies, dragonflies and praying mantis. There is a beautiful, spiraling relationship with the crickets and the circadian beings, as these harmonious relationships not only keep the rhythms of the planet steady and balanced but also have an amazing ability to heighten the vibrational nature of space and time.

Extraordinary ET water beings have also come to your planet, helping to restore the oceans and waterways. They have wonderful communication with the whales and dolphins, corresponding easily through sound vibrations and frequency shifts. ET "residences" remain deep within the waters of Earth, with crafts that can travel through both water and air and are often seen on the horizons of oceans and great lakes.

Humanoid beings, like Pleiadians, Sirians and Arcturians, are working closely with Earth and, indeed, many humans have close relationships with them. The highly evolved, vibratory level of their consciousness fields can change the color of the outer layer of the body, as it is a luminous light material. And so, many walk among you with only slight differences in appearance; however, when this is not in one's frame of reality, it is very easy to simply overlook what is right before you! There are also *off-planet humans* here to help usher in the New Age of Consciousness. They come from star civilizations that have made the transition from a technological/ego-centered phase to a highly evolved, advanced culture of humans in fifth dimensional consciousness. No doubt you have met them, or maybe you are just waking up to being one!

Advanced Energy Beings of higher-dimensional levels will become more apparent as the new *Spirit Teachers* of the human race.

Classrooms of the future will be holographic in nature and journeying in frequencies of consciousness will be the main modality for learning. The energetic field of Unity Consciousness will provide the new *teaching temple*, as the "freeways" for mapping cosmic instruction can only be found there.

Earth's atmosphere will reveal increased visual contact as human communities of High-Heart frequencies and expanded consciousness gather under the stars at night. Cohesive communal energy will create beacons of illumination to form "landing fields" in the sky and on the ground for star crafts. Contemporary theaters will be the crafted designs in the sky created by the dance with human consciousness and star being presence. The exalted energetic frequencies of the High-Heart will be the only admission ticket required for cosmic voyages to the outer rims of the galactic starlight-spirals. Finally, you may see the planet in all her beauty and know what we have known for eons of time...Earth is quite extraordinary and magnificent!

Various types of ET communication will increase exponentially, partly because it is a time of the Great Disclosure and partly to help you accelerate the opening of your *Soul Sensory Modalities*. We are utilizing these higher sensory modalities, like hearing, seeing, intuiting and telepathy, to communicate with you. Listen attentively and note changes in the sounds that abound around you. Look carefully and see the wisps of mist and contours of materialized energy, and know that **we** are coming closer to you through interdimensional corridors. Electronic anomalies and electromagnetic irregularities will be a common occurrence as human instruments are utilized as transmission devices. Approaching waves of synchronicities will foretell a crafted ship coming ever so close. The manifestation of the spiraling relationship between elevated ET beings and the great Mother Earth will be known and seen, and this will pave the lighted-golden path for the human species to follow.

Humans will open their intuitive channels and feel deep vibrations of the invisible world beckoning. *Extraterrestrial communication will become totally dependent on the human species' ability to create and sustain a higher vibrational field in which to meet them.* I believe you are familiar with the saying, "Build the field and they will come." Stay aligned with the High-Heart of the 5D self to create the higher-dimensional field in which you can commune together in lighted consciousness. We are here on Earth now more than you know. You have already created an energetic consciousness field and the fertile living air. Simply call us and we will come closer and, when you are breathing this fruited air of the Fifth Dimension, we will walk together in the lands of the New Dawn and the One Unity Breath.

Great ships in the Light Circle surrounding Earth will be the gathering grounds for the "United Nations" of Cosmic Civilizations, and many of you will be Earth ambassadors to this venture. You already are in the starlit, ethereal realms…do you remember?

Finally, advanced ET cultures will be able to share their technological know-how, which will aid in the restructuring of time and space on Earth. New solutions will be born out of the unified efforts of these conjoining endeavors with your galactic neighbors. New technologies will be offered and the problems of today will be relegated to the history books of tomorrow. Peace and harmonious symphonies of sounded frequencies will be heard across the globe and the spinning of time/space will open miraculous stargates to other lands and other realities. The mysteries will indeed become revelations of cosmic proportions!

EARTH

As you are surrounded by light emanating from the star-soul temple within, you will bring that light to all living beings and resonate with the same energy within them. Thus, you will be part of the wave of radiating light that will change the face of the Earth. The beautiful Earth Being will begin to grow new foods, and advanced resources will abound as part of the new dawning of health and wellbeing. There will no longer be species preying upon other species, as there will be abundance for all. And, you will be astounded by the aid you will receive from the trees, plants, animals and mineral queendom on Earth.

These new templates, consisting of nurturing frequencies, will guarantee that hunger, war, poverty and death will only be found in ancient textbooks as a reminder of where the Earth and her inhabitants have come from. No longer will there be divisions and separations or hierarchy of worthiness of life. Instead, all creatures, small and large, will share the lands of the planet in harmonious, cooperative and regenerative ways. Animals will work together to offer each other synergetic, life-producing methods and trees will signal when Earth's balance has been disrupted. Trees will also offer a new language of life and light as humans begin to honor their gateways to the beyond. Whales and dolphins will take their rightful place and design new ways of saving the planet's waterways. You will ride on the wings of the winged beings and surf on the backs of the water beings. Earth's soil will embrace you with a soothing energy bed fostering high health and balanced living. Humans will be able to breathe in the sounds of nature, as if the sounds themselves are the newly oxygenated giving substance of life. It will be understood that all of life is connected and so there will be a cooperative joining of forces for a higher ideal…that is yet to be revealed!

The most magnificent Earth Being, in her expansive consciousness, will communicate with other planetary beings, thus bringing new designs for Cosmic Unity. Divine Source will be seen in every sphere of life, as all living beings on Earth will be in sync with the unity breath of harmony and joy. As a result, Divine Source will shower Earth with the deep resonation of illuminated love and nurture the Spirit Temples of all living life.

Magnificence

Once more I say to you, be your Magnificence! Your Magnificence is simply to vibrate in the higher template of your Soul Being. It is your very Soul Light. It is the grand station where all connections to the inner and outer worlds meet, and the gateway to the stars and all that live there. The *Cosmic Synchronistic Web* is in full vibrant resonation and channels are open for travel within this temple of Magnificence. It is your deep connection with Source Spark that lies in the inner temple of You. The frequency of Magnificence defeats all previously veiled programs of diminishment. You are not those programs! Let the shields be dissolved so that the *lighted-soul* can see and be that grand illumination in the world. Your Soul Light is a divine template holding the fuel for all multidimensional expansion. It is your Source blueprint connecting to the irradiated Universe.

Be Magnificent and release the energetic fabric of your power-full, joy-full, heart-full, star-full, soul-full Self. Remember, what you see, hear, feel and touch in the higher multidimensional realms is only realized through your magnificent energetic body that lies in the core of your Soul Light. *Everything that is beautiful, sumptuous and illuminated in the world around you is a reflection of the Magnificent template within.* Without the vibrant resonation that arises from this inner Soul-lit fabric, the universal sacred dance of the Figure 8 would simply be motionless without spirit or luster. The miracle of birth and the magic of nature's elegance could not be seen or heard without the echoing inspiration that resides in this sacred chamber. Simply put, all roads to the mysteries and magic of the Synchronistic Cosmic Universe emanate from the Magnificent template within.

Congratulations, for it is already happening. Now, let your higher *SSM* show you what had previously been invisible and then share what has become visible with the All of the World. *As one positive thought can change the molecular structure of water, so the Magnificent Soul-Self can reverberate change to the entire planet and beyond!*

THE BEGINNING

As you embrace these written words and allow the liquid flow of their vibrational essences to awaken within, your inner cosmic circuitry begins lighting up and leaping into fifth dimensional consciousness. All of your experiences within these Cosmic pages are, in fact, a manifestation of your expanding Cosmic/Soul Self. The jubilant-self within is calling you. All lighted paths lead to the "knowing." You have experienced the crossing point of the cosmic mysteries and entered the vast, dimensional landscape of starlit consciousness. I have not said anything that is not within your most magnificent Soul Matrix. I have simply coaxed the openings, released the remembrances and allowed the whisperings of the Soul-Lighted Path.

You are a light worker and star sojourner and, as such, you are at a pinnacle point not only in this life but also within your entire Soul Matrix. This is an extraordinary, unparalleled time for your evolution. It will transform everything that is to come both within you and without you. When you imagine cities of the future and the landscapes of tomorrow, know you have already created them, as they stand bright with unimaginable light. Your imagination simply becomes the path by which you can travel to that dimensional realm where you have already spent much time creating and making anew. You have already prepared for the New Dawn...don't you see? You are simply clearing the debris that has littered and disguised the illuminated passages you have already built. There is more synchronicity than you can quite comprehend...for in a great life such as this there has been much preparation. You are well equipped with the perfect blueprint that maps this star journey into the multidimensional realms of All That Is.

Trust this is already within you and let these words simply open the guarded gates, bringing forth a tremendous light source both from your grand Soul Matrix and Divine Source itself. This time is most amazing, not just for what you are doing upon the Earth but what you are doing within the whole of your Soul Matrix. The leap to the next dimensional realm is Now...and this produces the new generation of fabricating the lighted ribbons of Consciousness for sixth dimensional Awareness.

Oh, did I say how this is affecting the Cosmos? Oh me, oh my... new light is being born...new energetic fields lifting up...thus, bringing elevated potentialities to the Universal Flow of life. High-frequency bands of illumination swirl and spiral into ssacred forms of Cosmic Oneness, Unity and Love...causing the heartbeat of the Universe to be heard in far-reaching lands, sparking life and love where there was none. You are Source Spark birthing Source Light.

This is not The End; it is truly The Beginning!

MEEAH LA (LOVE TO YOU)
ZAZAR

Made in the USA
Middletown, DE
16 July 2021

44146082R00126